BUSINESS OPPORTUNITIES IN PENANG, MALAYSIA

I HIGHLY RECOMMEND this volume to those considering investments in Penang, Malaysia, or in competing growth centres in Asia. This Business Study Mission report combines data from on-site inspections and secondary sources to provide broad coverage of topics such as labour markets, infrastructure, legal and tax issues, and business climate. While the focus here is on Penang, readers with a more general interest in Asia may find the analyses useful in evaluating other markets. Speeches (by Dr. Koh Tsu Koon, Chief Minister of Penang, and by others) included in the text provide insights into the thinking of regional government officials. This report provides a valuable tool for business executives, entrepreneurs, government officials and students.

PROF. THOMAS MCINISH, USA

COMPREHENSIVE AND OBJECTIVE, the book offers a broad-based overview of the prevalent business climate and market conditions, growth potential of and limitations to doing business in Penang, an understanding of which is crucial to achieving business results. A very readable and useful reference for the investor.

MARY PHIPPS, KPMG PEAT MARWICK, PENANG, MALAYSIA

Titles in the Nanyang Business Report Series

Business Opportunities in Penang, Malaysia

Business Opportunities in Sichuan Province, China

Business Opportunities in India

Business Opportunities in the Philippines

Business Opportunities in Myanmar

Business Opportunities in the Yangtze River Delta, China

For further enquiries, information or feedback on the series, please write to the Editor at e-mail: prenhall@singnet.com.sg or Simon & Schuster (Asia) Pte Ltd, 317 Alexandra Road, #04-01 IKEA Building, Singapore 159965.

NANYANG BUSINESS REPORT SERIES

Business Opportunities in Penang, Malaysia

Edited by

Tan Teck Meng (Dean)
Low Aik Meng (Vice Dean and Director of MBA Programme)
Chew Soon Beng (Head, Applied Economics)
John J. Williams (Chief Coordinator, Business Study Mission)
Tan Khee Giap (Coordinator, Business Study Mission)

Nanyang Technological University
Singapore

Prentice Hall
Singapore New York London Toronto Sydney Tokyo

First published 1996 by
Prentice Hall
Simon & Schuster (Asia) Pte Ltd
317 Alexandra Road
#04-01 IKEA Building
Singapore 159965

Printed in Singapore

1 2 3 4 5 00 99 98 97 96

ISBN 0-13-713323-5
ISBN 0-13-267907-8 (pbk)

Prentice Hall International (UK) Limited, *London*
Prentice Hall of Australia Pty. Limited, *Sydney*
Prentice Hall Canada Inc., *Toronto*
Prentice Hall Hispanoamericana, *S.A., Mexico*
Prentice Hall of India Private Limited, *New Delhi*
Prentice Hall of Japan, Inc., *Tokyo*
Editora Prentice Hall do Brasil, Ltda., *Rio de Janeiro*
Prentice Hall, Inc., *Upper Saddle River, New Jersey*

CONTENTS

BANKING AND LABOUR MARKETS

LABOUR LEGISLATION AND DEVELOPMENT

OVERVIEW OF SUCCESS FACTORS

SPEECH HIGHLIGHTS

ABOUT THE EDITORS

TAN TECK MENG is Professor and Dean at the Nanyang Business School. Since joining academia in the early 1970s, Professor Tan has combined his university responsibilities with extensive consultancy work, largely in the field of accountancy. He holds senior positions on a number of institutional boards and committees in Singapore including the Accounting and Auditing Services Working Group of the Economic Committee, the Public Accountants Board, the Board of Directors of Singapore Reinsurance Corporation Limited, the Institute of Certified Public Accountants of Singapore (ICPAS) Annual Report Award Competition Committee and the Income Tax Board of Review. Professor Tan is founding Director of the Entrepreneurship Development Centre (ENDEC) and in 1992 was elected to the Board of Governors of the MIT Sloan School of Management Society for Senior Executives. He is a council member of the ICPAS.

LOW AIK MENG is Associate Professor and Director of the MBA programme at the Nanyang Business School. He worked for five years as an accountant and an internal auditor before joining academia in 1975. He was Vice-Dean of the Faculty of Accountancy and Business Administration at the National University of Singapore until he joined the Nanyang Technological University in 1987. He is currently Vice-Dean at the Nanyang Business School and has been the Director of its very successful MBA Programme since its inception in 1991. Under his leadership, the MBA Programme has been building a network of contacts with businesses and government bodies in Singapore and overseas. He spearheads the thrice-yearly Business Study Missions which are an integral part of the MBA Programme. Associate Professor Low continues to be active in the accountancy profession and serves on several committees in the Institute of Certified Public Accountants of Singapore.

CHEW SOON BENG is Associate Professor and Head of the Applied Economics Division at the Nanyang Business School. He is also the Director of the Asian Commerce and Economics Studies Centre (ACES) which conducts Mandarin executive programmes for senior officials from China and tourism management programmes for senior officials from Vietnam. Dr. Chew has been a consultant to the International Labour Organization and the Asian Development Bank. He is author of, *inter alia*, *Small Firms in Singapore* (Oxford University Press, 1988), *Trade Unionism in Singapore* (McGraw Hill, 1990), and *The Employment-Driven Industrial Relations Regimes* (Avebury, 1995).

JOHN J. WILLIAMS is Associate Professor at the Nanyang Business School and Chief Coordinator of the MBA Business Study Mission programme. He has taught and carried out research projects in several countries including Canada, the U.S., Kenya and Singapore. Throughout the latter part of the 1980s, Dr. Williams served as Vice-Chairman and Chairman of the Final Accreditation Exam Board for the Society of Management Accountants of Canada, which admitted him as a Fellow in the Society in 1992. Although active in consulting for government agencies in the U.S. and Canada during this period, he has published extensively in leading academic and professional journals and he continues to pursue the study of emerging regional economies in the Asean region.

TAN KHEE GIAP is Senior Lecturer and Head of the Econometric Modeling Unit. Dr. Tan started as a treasury manager in the private sector upon completion of his PhD from the University of East Anglia, U.K. Prior to joining NTU, he taught at the National University of Singapore. He serves as a consultant to several MNCs and banks. His research publications are in the areas of macro- economics and monetary economics. He is currently doing research on an Asean macroeconomic link model with the Trade Development Board of Singapore and credit card business with VISA International.

PREFACE

The Master of Business Administration (MBA) programme of the Nanyang Business School at Nanyang Technological University requires participants to complete a Business Study Mission (BSM) before graduation. The purpose of these visits to other countries is to expose MBA participants to business opportunities and the realities of doing business in cultural environments different from Singapore.

The contents of this book are based on the business reports from the five-day BSM to Penang, Malaysia in February 1994. Collectively, they focus on important business opportunities in Penang, the complementarity between Singapore and Penang in this respect, and the critical role that Penang enjoys in the Indonesian-Malaysian-Thailand Growth Triangle (IMT-GT). The latter economic zone constitutes one of the most affluent regional economic units emerging in Asia today. This growth triangle is regarded by Kenichi Ohmae as a primary example of a borderless economy that is reshaping global markets.

In amassing the information, this book is privileged by the richness of primary information obtained from different input sources which included significant business forums, speeches and interactive discussions with top-ranking government Ministers and leading executives from the business community, formal seminars, and site visits to major corporations and agencies. These multiple perspectives provide an understanding of the salient features of the economic climate for any potential investor, large or small.

While the audience of potential investors is far-reaching, including both the private sector and foreign government agencies, the book also provides a source of resource materials for research and feasibility studies. Moreover, it provides a benchmark for evaluating and assessing the economic gains and prosperity of the region in the years to follow. In addition, the editors hope that other professional organisations and tertiary educational institutions can benefit from the insights gained and presented here on the business opportunities available in Penang and its surrounding economic zone.

Editors:
TAN Teck Meng
LOW Aik Meng
CHEW Soon Beng
John J. WILLIAMS
TAN Khee Giap

ACKNOWLEDGEMENTS

We wish to express our appreciation first to the speakers, the Right Honourable Dr. Koh Tsu Koon, Chief Minister of Penang, the Right Honourable Datuk Dr. Ibrahim Saad, Deputy Chief Minister of Penang, and Dr. Cham Tao Soon, President of NTU for their lucid summaries on the importance of this BSM together with understanding macroeconomic policies and strategies in the region.

Special thanks are extended to Yg Bhg Dato'Noor Ahmad Mokhtar Haniff, General Manager, Penang Development Corporation (PDC) and to Mrs. B. J. Yeang, General Manager, Industrial and Trade Division, PDC, for her untiring briefings and extraordinary knowledge on the Penang economy. For the forum guests and seminar speakers, thanks to Dr. Min Tang, Senior Economist, Asian Development Bank; En. Manmohan Singh, Malaysia Development Authority, Penang; Mr. Patrick Pillai, ISIS; K. Gopalan, PDC; Mr. Sivagnanam, MEF; and Mr. Terence Chan, Managing Director, CAD-IT consultants.

We are grateful to CAD-IT Consultants, Eng Technology, and Tri-M/Sekum Engineering for hosting the site visits for our 40-member delegation. Thanks also go to all of the contributors of the main chapters in this book and to the MBA Office, Nanyang Business School, for providing the secretarial and administrative support in bringing this volume to completion. We value the efforts of Prentice Hall, our publisher, and the guidance of Lam Wai Ling, Managing Editor, in structuring the book.

THE PENANG ECONOMY

Chapter 1

Emerging Investment Opportunities between Singapore and Penang: An Overview of Perspectives

BY
TAN Teck Meng
LOW Aik Meng
CHEW Soon Beng
John J. WILLIAMS
TAN Khee Giap

INTRODUCTION

THERE IS VIRTUAL unanimity that potential business linkages between Singapore and Penang can be approached from different perspectives. Clearly, then, one important question is which of the many significant perspectives should be included within the context of a Business Study Mission to Penang.

One important consideration, it seems, is embedded in the structure of industrial enterprise in Singapore and the educational objective underpinning the MBA programme at Nanyang Technological University. Given the strong entrepreneurial emphasis and focus on the role of small business in our MBA programme, is there justification for concentrating on this sector of the economy as opposed to multinational corporations or government linked companies, per se?

Broadly speaking, Singapore has amassed a mix of multinational corporations, government linked companies, local enterprise and entrepreneurship. The 1960s and early 1970s witnessed the establishment of a strong manufacturing base while recent years have yielded an infusion of capital and technologically intensive activities which extend into the service and commerce sector of the economy. According to statistics released by the Economic Development Board (EDB) (May 1993), there are approximately 80,000 business establishments in the Singapore economy and just under 90% of this aggregate comprises medium and small local enterprises. Even more striking is that more than one half of the total value added in Singapore emanates from these sources. Not surprisingly, approximately 65% of the labour force is anchored in these businesses (see Table 1-1).

TABLE 1-1
Local Enterprise Data for 1990

Sector	Non-manufacturing	Commerce	Service	Total
Number of Businesses				
SMEs	2,867	40,616	25,969	69,452
Local Large	67	447	382	896
Other	769	2,214	6,735	9,718
Total	3,703	43,277	33,086	80,066
Number of Employees				
SMEs	121,666	170,611	101,696	393,973
Local Large	30,486	59,345	124,579	214,410
Other	199,522	49,844	73,290	322,656
Total	351,674	279,800	299,565	931,039
Value Added ($m)				
SMEs	4,312.2	4,336.6	4,358.9	13,007.7
Local Large	1,974.8	2,443.4	10,095.0	14,513.2
Other	15,319.8	4,866.1	3,954.0	24,139.9
Total	21,606.8	11,646.1	18,407.9	51,660.8

Source: Adapted from Singapore Economic Development Board, *Growing with Enterrise: A National Effort*, May 1993.

While Singapore has prudently attracted capital, labour and technology from outside its boundaries to facilitate this mix, there has been a continual push on the demand side, not only to sustain profits, but to create new market opportunities decisively and innovatively. Government policy is clearly dedicated towards promoting more regionalisation and globalisation but, even more importantly, special efforts are being directed towards assisting local entrepreneurship to expand and internationalise.

Evidence here can be found in the EDB's SME Master Plan which was inaugurated in 1989 and which received further support in 1993 under the Ministry of Finance to promote overseas businesses. There are a number of individual financial schemes which the EDB has reported at nearly $3,362 million. In particular, nearly 77% of this amount has been apportioned to the Local Enterprise Finance loan scheme.[1] Clearly, there are strong initiatives in existence to propel local companies into overseas markets such as Malaysia, and Penang in particular, where economies of labour and space are an excellent fit for Singapore's entrepreneurial talent. In fact, information released by Singapore's Department of Statistics (1990) indicates that over 22% of Singapore's direct foreign investment abroad is located in Malaysia. And, in order to give some sense of distribution, only 19% of the $1,663 million invested by Singapore in Malaysia is attributable to the manufacturing sector.[2]

Apart from these few brief indicators of entrepreneurial talent and potential existing in Singapore, there are other examples of efforts to expand the economic ties and investment opportunities between Singapore and Penang. As Dr. Cham noted in his closing speech (see p. 155), a seminar devoted specifically to the promotion of investment opportunities in Penang was organised in Singapore in July 1993. And, on 21 January 1994, the Lee Kuan Yew Exchange Fellows Programme featured the Deputy Minister of Penang, Dr. Ibrahim Saad, who candidly spelled out the ideal investment location features of Penang.

It seems fitting, then, to suggest that ample reasons existed to adopt an entrepreneurial perspective in the BSM to Penang. However, to properly evaluate what Penang has to offer, it is necessary to address the larger economic expansion that is impacting Penang in the form of economic relationships and alliances with neighbouring countries. Finally, it is appropriate to evaluate the potential business synergisms which may emerge from assessing the complementary strengths of Penang and Singapore. It is these latter considerations that dominate the remainder of this book.

---

1 Singapore, Economic Development Board, *Growing with Enterprise: A National Effort*, May 1993.

2 Singapore, Department of Statistics, *Singapore's Investment Abroad*, February 1993, Singapore National Printers.

PENANG'S EXTERNAL ECONOMY: A NEW GROWTH TRIANGLE

The term "growth triangle" was coined by the Prime Minister of Singapore, Goh Chok Tong, in the latter part of 1989 to denote a regional area of economic alliance among Singapore, southern Johor and the island of Batam in Indonesia. Since then, of course, the concept has been used to describe a number of regional economic alliances among ASEAN countries. Chapter 2 differentiates these economic entities from traditional trading blocs and export processing zones and elaborates on the emergence of the Indonesia-Malaysia-Thailand Growth Triangle (IMT-GT).

The IMT-GT is important in the assessment of economic activity in Penang because the latter forms the central nucleus of the economic linkages within this region. Based on this understanding, Chapter 2 sets forth the economic complementarities of the IMT-GT which include labour cost issues, export trade, land availability, mobility of labour, and investment, before dealing with significant constraints. This discussion sets the stage for exploring growth opportunities in Penang. The perspectives considered in this chapter provide a fundamental insight for any investment entry into Penang including the appropriate networking focus to ensure entrepreneurial success.

In comprehending the information contained in Chapter 2, it is worthwhile to recall the speech by the Deputy Chief Minister of Penang contained in the forward to this volume. It will be observed that not only is there political support and commitment for the contents of Chapter 2 but, patently, one obtains a better understanding of the IMT-GT in the context of globalisation – an emerging feature of business activity that even regional entrepreneurs must be cognisant of in considering new investment opportunities.

PENANG'S FUNCTIONAL ATTRIBUTES

The Chief Minister of Penang has clearly indicated that the future success of Penang and, indeed, its current success, is located in a mix of diversified industry and commerce. One component is the manufacturing sector and this sector will require ancillary and support businesses to facilitate the growth and expansion of the MNCs. This is a prime focus for entrepreneurial linkages with Singapore because high value-added resources and capital are essential for the type of expansion required by the MNCs. It also should be noted that Penang must develop these linkages in its role as a hub for the local economy, as a centre for the emergence of expanded economic activity from the IMT-GT, and as a centre for expanding new ASEAN and world markets.

In order to reach the targets within these three different types of economic alliances, Penang must offer foreign investors a complete package of incentives and attractions. Hence, Chapter 3 describes some of these qualities including infrastructure facilities, labour force characteristics, stability of government and general quality of life issues. Since incentives are such a critical pull factor in this respect, Chapter 4 focuses specifically on incentives geared to local enterprise, joint ventures, and direct foreign investment that have largely been implemented and controlled by the PDC.

Tax considerations are indispensable to any business investment decision and potential benefits here in terms of cash flows and profits often can be the deciding factor. Thus, Chapter 5 looks at some key comparative differences in the tax structure between Penang and Singapore. Among others, issues of corporate tax rates, special capital cost allowances, repatriation of profits and export incentives are discussed.

Evaluating business opportunities nearly always invokes some assessment of the host's banking system and financial markets. Since Penang is not the capital of Malaysia, it would be unfair to expect it to duplicate the role played by Kuala Lumpur. Nonetheless, it is important to consider Penang's role more in the sense of a three-pronged economic hub as alluded to earlier rather than as a distinct and independent regional financial centre. These issues and some of the consequent implications for Singaporean investment are highlighted in Chapter 6.

Managing the labour force, industrial employment turnover, labour regulations and programmes to upgrade workforce skills and productivity, are essential economic features that potential investors must assess. Business people know that high-tech endeavours, for example, must be supported by the requisite level of skilled labour. Otherwise, production efficiencies and market opportunities will not be realised nor will the initial incentives for business expansion be realised. Therefore, the labour infrastructure that exists in Penang is one of the more important factors that must be assessed.

To begin with, Chapter 7 discloses some important information, in general terms, on the nature and make-up of Penang's labour force, employment turnover rates and wage costs. Not surprisingly, Penang's wage cost structure relative to Singapore is a major pull factor in analysing investment opportunities. At the same time, the stability of the labour force over time, both with respect to collective agreements and wage increases, is an important factor and, thus, becomes the subject matter of Chapter 8. Finally, some of the assistance schemes and government support programmes available for upgrading labour skills and enhancing long term productivity are discussed in Chapter 9. Where it is prudent and informative, each of these three chapters attempts to contrast and compare the similarities of the labour issues in Penang with those that are to be found in Singapore.

However, since labour is only one aspect of the Penang economy which is important to potential investors, a more comprehensive and macro perspective is offered in Chapter 10. Here, the areas of competition and complementarity that present themselves in a Penang-Singapore connection are illustrated. Finally, Chapter 11 deals with an overview and synthesis of the preceding chapters. In attempting to summarise the complex and diverse issues addressed throughout the volume, important questions for *future* consideration and assessment by potential investors are raised in this final chapter. Hopefully, a return BSM at some future date can assess the relevance of these concerns.

Chapter 2

Indonesia-Malaysia-Thailand Growth Triangle: An Overview and Policy Strategies

BY
Min TANG
Myo THANT*

INTRODUCTION

RECENTLY, SEVERAL LOCALISED economic cooperation zones known as "Growth Triangles" have emerged in Asia. Unlike trading blocs, which require nationwide institutions and administrative arrangements, growth triangles usually involve only portions of countries and can be established at a lower cost and in less time than formal trading blocs. A growth triangle is also different from an export processing zone by involving the participation of more countries and more sectoral activities, such as tourism, natural and human resource development, and joint infrastructure development, aside

* *Economists, Economics and Development Resource Center, Asian Development Bank.* *The authors wish to thank Ms. A. Z. Pardo and Ms. P. C. Baysa for their invaluable assistance. The authors are also grateful for the invaluable comments of the MBA Business Mission to Penang from Nanyang Technological University of Singapore.* *The views expressed in this paper are those of the authors and do not necessarily reflect the views and policies of the Asian Development Bank.*

from the trade and investment activities which are the core of export processing zones.

The term "growth triangle" came into common use after the former Deputy Prime Minister of Singapore, Goh Chok Tong, used it in December 1989, to describe the sub-regional economic cooperation involving Singapore, southern Johor, and Batam island in Indonesia. The economic cooperation between Hong Kong, Taipei, China, and the southern part of the People's Republic of China (PRC) (mainly parts of Guangdong and Fujian provinces) has been referred to as the southern China Growth Triangle. The Tumen River Area Development Programme, which includes parts of Jilin province in the PRC, Siberia in Russia, and the Democratic People's Republic of Korea, has also been described as another growth triangle (see Table 2-1).

Encouraged by the success of the southern China and the Johor-Singapore-Riau Growth Triangle, the governments of Indonesia, Malaysia and Thailand decided to establish a new growth triangle in southern Thailand, northern Malaysia and the Sumatra area of Indonesia in July 1993, in order to enhance economic cooperation and increase social welfare in the region. This paper first describes the basic characteristics of this growth triangle, commonly known as the Indonesia-Malaysia-Thailand Growth Triangle (IMT-GT). Second, it examines the complementarities in the triangle. Finally, the paper identifies the opportunities and challenges of the IMT-GT.

CHARACTERISTICS OF THE INDONESIA-MALAYSIA-THAILAND GROWTH TRIANGLE

The Indonesia-Malaysia-Thailand Growth Triangle consists of the states of northern Sumatra and Aceh in Indonesia, the four states of Perak, Penang, Kedah and Perlis in northern Malaysia and the five provinces of Songkhla, Satun, Yala, Narathiwat and Pattani in southern Thailand (see Figure 2-1). The total area of the IMT-GT constitutes 180,000 sq. kms. with a total population of about 22 million. The Indonesian part of the triangle is by far the largest with two-thirds of the area and the total population of the triangle. Northern Malaysia and southern Thailand contribute 18% and 12% of the area and 22% and 13% of the population, respectively.

The three sub-regions in the IMT-GT possess considerable resources and growth potential. On the Malaysian side, the major urban centres are George Town and Butterworth in Penang and Ipoh in Perak. Industrial growth has been dramatic over the last decade and the area has developed rapidly. However, despite the recent industrialisation, the north-western states are among the least affluent in Malaysia. Kedah, Perlis and Perak have a lower per capita GDP than almost all of the other states in Malaysia. Penang is also experiencing a shortage of both skilled and unskilled labour.

TABLE 2-1
Growth Triangles in Asia

	South China-Hong Kong-Taipei-China	**Singapore-Johor-Riau**	**Tumen River Area Development**	**Indonesia-Malaysia-Thailand**	**Brunei-Indonesia-Malaysia-Philippines**
Date of Inception	Early 1980s	1989/90	1991	1993	1994
Participating Areas	Guangdong and Fujian Province of PRC, Hong Kong, Taipei, China.	Riau Province of Indonesia, Johor of Malaysia, Singapore.	Jilin Province of China, northern part of North Korea, far east part of Russia.	Southern Thailand, northern Malaysia, north Sumatra and Aceh of Indonesia.	Brunei, north Sulawesi, east and west Kalimantan of Indonesia, Sarawak, Sabah and Labuan of Malaysia, Mindanao of Philippines.
Area	430,000 sq. km.	20,000 sq. km.		180,000 sq. km.	1,000,000 sq. km.
Population	120 million	6 million		22 million	20 million
Focus	Export of labour-intensive goods and economic development zones.	Export of manufactured goods.	Infrastructure development, free trade zones and joint natural resource development.	Expansion of trade and investment; Joint development of infrastructure and tourism; cooperation in agriculture and fishery and increasing factor mobility.	Sectoral cooperation; Infrastructure development; mineral, forest and marine resource development; trade and investment increasing factor.

FIGURE 2-1
Indonesia-Malaysia-Thailand Growth Triangle

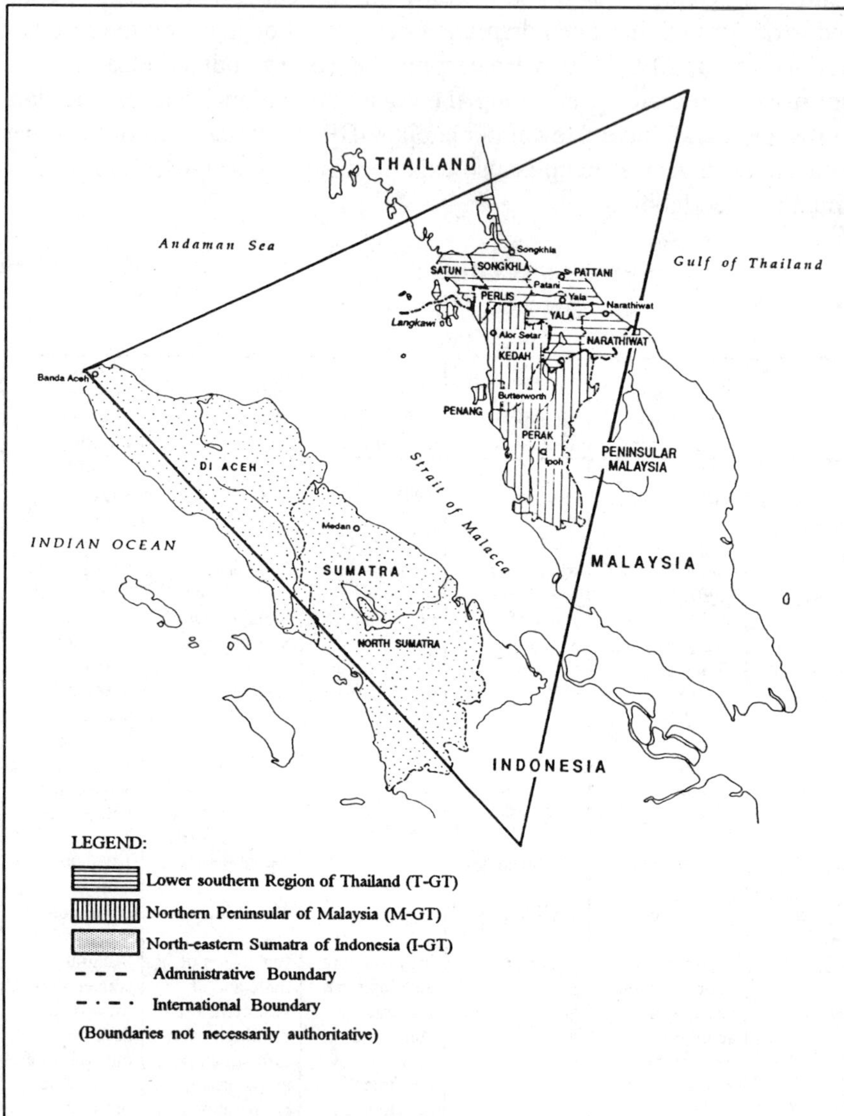

In southern Thailand, the area is traditionally agricultural with rubber plantations in the uplands and padi on the irrigated plains. There are significant industrial developments in Songkhla and Haadyai. A deep seaport is located at Pattani in the Gulf of Thailand as well as industrial estates. A network of main and minor access roads serves the region and connects to five border crossing points. A new east-west road is to be constructed which will open the immediate border area to development.

Northern Sumatra is predominantly agricultural with two-thirds of the workforce directly engaged in farm activities. Products from the area represent approximately one-quarter of the national agricultural exports. Due to the completion of large irrigation projects, agriculture projects have boomed in Aceh. The industrial activities are agro-based, such as rubber-based industries. Basic and metal industries include aluminum and other metals most of which are manufactured for export.

The economic performance of the IMT-GT area has been very strong in the past. The Indonesian part of the triangle grew at an average rate of 7% in the period from 1985 to 1988. In southern Thailand, GDP growth was as high as 7.2% per annum during 1985–89. Though the per capita income of northern Malaysia is well above that of the other two parts of the growth triangle, the GDP growth rate was 5% per annum which was much lower (see Table 2-2).

Economic linkages within the IMT-GT area have a long history. The geographical proximity and cultural ties among Peninsular Malaysia, lower southern Thailand and northern Sumatra, has led to a strong trade relationship. Northern Sumatra's exports to Malaysia account for over 20% of total Indonesian exports to Malaysia. The shared border between southern Thailand and northern Malaysia has also resulted in a large volume of trade. In addition, however, there is an active and growing illegal trade in the border areas.

The IMT-GT has attracted large scale foreign direct investment (FDI). It was reported that the five provinces of southern Thailand have witnessed an upsurge in investment and manufacturing activity since 1989. In particular, more than one-half of the approved investment projects have been allocated to Songkhla province. The majority of these projects are in seafood, agro-processing, latex and rubber goods. Malaysia is the leading country for investment and the major investors include Taipei, China, Japan, Hong Kong and Singapore. In northern Malaysia, four states have accounted for almost half of national FDI approvals in recent years, mostly in Penang, followed by Perak, Kedah and Perlis. Investments are concentrated in the electrical and electronics products. The major sources of FDI are France, Taipei, China, Japan and the U.S. Investments from Thailand and Indonesia are very minimal. In recent years, northern Malaysia has undergone an industrial restructuring. Penang is experiencing a significant decline in investment, particularly in labour-intensive industries. In northern Sumatra, the FDI projects are mostly related to the plantations. There also have been some heavy industrial projects in Aceh. European countries and the U.S. accounted for most of the FDI in northern Sumatra. Finally, there have been some investment projects from Thailand and Malaysia (Rao, 1994).

TABLE 2-2
Macroeconomics Data of Indonesia-Malaysia-Thailand Growth Triangle

Country/ Region	Total Population ('000) 1990	Area (km)	Population Density/km 1990	Average Annual Growth Rate of Population (%) 1980-91	Real GDP (US$ Bn) 1988	Real GDP per Capita (US)*
Indonesia	179,380	1,904,600	94	1.8	59.312	337.78
Northern Sumatra	13,667	127,070	108	-	3.455	
					5.525	404.80
North Sumatra	10,252	71,680	143	2.1	-	-
Aceh	3,415	55,390	62	3.0	-	-
Malaysia	17,760	329,800	54	2.6	25.318	1,494.57
Northern Malaysia	4,658	32,256	144	1.6	5.239	1,148.50
Perak	2,040	21,005	97	-	-	-
Penang	1,133	1,031	1,099	-	-	-
Kedah	1,301	9,425	138	-	-	-
Perlis	184	795	231	-	-	-
Thailand	58,080	513,100	109	1.9	72.307	1,247.77
Southern Thailand	2,840	20,809	136	2.0	2.200	769.00
Satun	217	2,479	88	-	-	-
Pattani	566	1,940	292	-	-	-
Songkhla	1,148	7,394	155	-	-	-
Yala	364	4,521	81	-	-	-
Narathiwat	545	4,475	122	-	-	-

Notes: * The base year of the real GDP values for Indonesia is 1988, for Malaysia 1978 and for Thailand, 1988.

The average exchange rates of 1988 for the three countries are:

- 1,685.70 Indonesian rupiah per US$.
- 2.6188 Malaysian ringgit per US$.
- 25.294 Thai baht per US$.

Source: Naseem (1994), Table 3.

ECONOMIC COMPLEMENTARITIES OF IMT-GT

The foundation of a growth triangle is economic complementarity among the parties involved which is derived from the parties' different stages of economic development or from differences in their factor endowments. In the southern China and Singapore-Johor-Riau triangles, there is both a fairly well-developed urbanised area as well as a less developed, low-income area. Hong Kong, Singapore, Taipei and China also have strong industrial sectors, well-developed financial markets, fairly advanced infrastructure facilities and a well-trained labour force. On the other hand, southern China, Johor and the Riau Islands have an ample supply of both labour and land. A redistribution of labour-intensive industries from the well-developed areas to the relatively less developed areas within the growth triangle would be mutually beneficial.

Strong economic complementarities are apparent in the IMT-GT. First, there is significant potential complementarity in terms of natural resource endowments. Among the three regions, northern Sumatra has the strongest natural resource base. It has substantial forest resources, oil and gas. It also has relatively unexploited offshore fishery reserves and a strong inland fishing industry. Moreover, there is a substantial surplus in food crops such as rice and vegetables in northern Sumatra. Turning to northern Malaysia, there are substantial reserves of limestone, dolomite and china clay, but there are shortages of land for resource-based activities as well as for petroleum and natural gas. In southern Thailand, there are abundant forestry reserves including vast rubberwood plantations. Mineral reserves such as tin, barite, chromium, kaolin and lead are also abundant.

Second, there is complementarity among the three sub-regions in terms of the extent of land scarcity. Northern Malaysia has a limited land area and it is experiencing a shortage of land for resource-based activities. Northern Sumatra and, to some extent the southern Triangle, both have substantial availability of land for agriculture and industrial activities. As a result, the land price is much higher in Malaysia than it is in the other two sub-regions. For example, the sale price of developed industrial land in Penang is more than twice as high as in the Yala of Thailand and northern Sumatra (see Table 2-3).

In terms of labour cost, northern Sumatra has a strong comparative advantage across the board (Table 2-4). Daily labour cost in this sub-

TABLE 2-3
Land Sale and Construction Costs

	Raw Industrial Land Sale Price (US$/m²)	Developed Industrial Land Sale Price (US$/m²)
Indonesia		
Northern Sumatra		$9.57–$28.70
Malaysia		
Kedah		$2.21–$19.23
Perak		$14.61–$23.85
Perlis		$13.45
Penang		$41.38–$51.75
Thailand		
Narathiwat	$3.70	$24.70
Songkhla	$24.70–$39.50	
Yala	$17.28–$24.70	

Source: Rao (1994), Table 3.2.

region is below US$2.00 while the rate is about four times higher in Penang, Malaysia. The minimum wage in Thailand is approximately US$4.00/day but the average unskilled labour rates in Yala and Songkhla are US$7.40 to US$8.70/day. The availability of labour is strong in northern Sumatra but northern Malaysia and southern Thailand are experiencing labour shortages (Rao, 1994).

There is also economic complementarity among the three regions in terms of the pattern of trade. North Sumatra has a strong comparative trade advantage in crude petroleum, oil and gas, plywood, vegetables and rubber products. Southern Thailand is strong in fish and fishery products, furniture and wood products. The comparative advantage of northern Malaysia dominates relatively high-skilled capital intensive products such as electrical apparatus and electronics. Northern Malaysia is also competitive in refined palm oil and processed wood.

It also should be pointed out that economic complementarities do not necessarily come from the parties which are geographically located in the growth triangle. The growth triangle is an open economic zone and it has an export-oriented structure. Economic benefits are derived by those areas which are not part of the triangle through engaging in trade and investment in the areas of the triangle. For example, in Shenzhen which is part of the southern China growth triangle, only one-half of the total FDI came from Hong Kong and Taipei in 1990. Economic complementarity among the parties located within the Tumen Delta itself are rather weak and capital is expected to come largely from Japan and the Republic of Korea, neither of which are physically located in the proposed triangle (Tang and Thant, 1993).

TABLE 2-4
Labour Costs and Other Characteristics

	Min. Wage for Unskilled Labour (US$/day)	Average Wage for Unskilled Labour (US$/day)	Average Wage for Skilled Labour (US$/day)	Average Wage for Technicians (US$/month)	Average Wage for Middle Management (US$/month)
Indonesia					
Aceh					
N. Sumatra	$1.48	$2.06	$3.35	$129.19	$216.31
Malaysia					
Kedah	no min. wage	$2.30–$6.92	$13.40	$329	
Perak	no min. wage	$3.46–$6.00	$13.38	$321	
Perlis	no min. wage	$2.50–$4.93	$10.08	$245	
Penang	no min. wage	$5.00–$8.58	$13.81	$341	$789 – $1,150
Thailand					
Narathiwat	$4.03				
Pattani	$4.03				
Satun	$4.03				
Songkhla	$4.03	$7.41	$13.20	$237 – $516	$632 – $790
Yala	$4.03	$8.70			

Note: Exchange rates used: B25.31 = US$1; M$2.60 = US$1; Rs2,090 = US$1. Malaysia wage rates, statutory fringe benefits and customary additions such as overtime allowance, bonus, incentive payments, transportation allowances, housing, shift and meal allowance, etc. Data is from Manpower Resource Study, 1993.

Source: Rao (1994), Table 3.1.

Since the output of IMT-GT is largely for export, and capital invested in the area comes mainly from the rest of the participating countries and other foreign countries, it is necessary to develop a broader view of economic complementarity. In particular, there are strong complementarities between the IMT-GT area and metropolitan areas of the participating countries such as Jakarta in Indonesia, Kuala Lumpur in

Malaysia and Bangkok in Thailand. Thus, huge business and investment opportunities can be identified from these areas.

OPPORTUNITIES AND CHALLENGES FOR IMT-GT

The establishment of IMT-GT presents both opportunities and challenges for the sub-regions. Its development will extend the frontier of prosperity in the sub-regions and will inject a powerful dynamic stimulus capable of bringing them into the mainstream of the regions' economic and social developments. First, the establishment of the triangle would enhance the prospects of development of more dynamic complementarities within the triangle. Southern Thailand and northern Sumatra consist predominantly of agricultural-based areas with a low share of manufacturing activities (5% in Thailand and 10% in Indonesia). On the other hand, Penang in northern Malaysia is the most industrialised part of the growth triangle. There is a huge potential for manufacturing and industrial development in these areas, particularly for an efficient, specialised agri-business and agro-processing industry development. Second, the IMT-GT contains a huge reservoir of marine and forest resources which represents a vast opportunity for productive cooperation among the three countries. Third, the establishment of the triangle would also benefit from the domestic and foreign investment inflows that have swept the region for over a decade.

OPPORTUNITIES FOR IMT-GT

In general, existing trade, investment, and labour flows, both formal and informal, in the Growth Triangle indicate that regional development is desirable and feasible. At the sectoral level, there are also vast opportunities for cooperation.

Regional Trade

Most of the intra-regional trade occurs across the common border of southern Thailand and northern Malaysia. Direct trading activities between southern Thailand and northern Sumatra seem to be rather weak. Trade between northern Malaysia and southern Sumatra is limited to traditional agricultural commodities although the development of energy resources and tree crops in northern Sumatra may change this condition (Naseem, 1994).

It is important to distinguish between trade which is based upon real economic complementarities, and trade which is driven by temporary policy differences and distortions. Much of the thriving trade across the Thailand-Malaysia border is driven by differences in import tariffs and price control policies. High duties provide the incentive for Thailand to import electrical and electronic products, used machinery, palm oil and cement from Malaysia; exports from Thailand consist mainly of rubber and food products. Other informal trade between Malaysia and Thailand, including rice, palm oil, and garments, is probably due to real complementarities in the form of production costs as well as to price controls and import quotas. Much the same is true for exports of vegetables and fruits from Indonesia to Malaysia and for fish to Thailand. These products can form a basis for triangle growth development.

It is also important to distinguish between large volume formal trade flows and border trade in which the latter occurs outside the formal system and is relatively small in volume. There is a thriving border trade in agricultural commodities between northern Sumatra and northern Malaysia which builds upon long-standing historical relationships. Northern Sumatra has been exporting fresh vegetables to Malaysia for many years. The further expansion and normalisation of this trade has been limited by an annual import quota imposed by Malaysia (which has now been increased to US$200 million) and lack of cold storage and other post-harvest handling and transport facilities in northern Sumatra. Although the trade in these and other products is currently small, it can become important for the development of the triangle region once barriers to trade and investment are removed.

Labour Mobility

As in the case of trade flows, labour flows between the sub-regions of the triangle also suggest the feasibility of further inter-regional growth and development. The importance of cross-border flows and general labour issues in the context of the growth triangle is two-fold. First, labour must be mobile to meet the urgent manpower requirements of such rapidly expanding economies as that of northern Malaysia. The terms and conditions under which such mobility is to operate must be clearly defined. Second, there must be an active human resource development effort so that domestic manpower can meet the needs of more capital-intensive and technologically skilled industry. This will allow highly labour-intensive operations to shift to labour surplus economies with low labour costs. Policies that control or restrict the flow of labour will have a direct impact on the movement of labour-intensive enterprises.

The acute labour shortage in Malaysia has been partially alleviated by the entry of labourers from Indonesia, Myanmar, the Philippines, Thailand, and elsewhere. The majority of these workers have been employed in agricultural plantations, fishing activities, construction and some agro-industrial processing. Approximately one-half of these workers are in Malaysia without work permits. While this low-cost labour force has preserved the competitiveness of Malaysian industry it has had a significant cost on public and social services and it has probably delayed the restructuring of Malaysian industry toward more capital-intensive, higher wage, production.

In response to demands by industry, the government of Malaysia has recently permitted the importation of technical and skilled labour to work toward the expansion of industry in Penang. The governments of Malaysia and Indonesia recently have signed a Memorandum of Understanding which will normalise the importation of Indonesian labour, subject to annual quotas and other conditions. While these are certainly steps in the right direction there is a great deal of ambivalence about labour policy and the speed at which Malaysia should be "exporting" labour-intensive industry. Facilitating the importation of labour can delay the restructuring of the economy and the migration of highly labour-intensive industry. This tendency is exacerbated by the fact that there are pockets of excess labour in Malaysia.

Investment

Trends in direct investment in the three sub-regions also indicate the feasibility of an enhanced growth triangle. There appears to be a significant increase in direct investment in southern Thailand within the growth triangle area. In the first ten months of 1993, 27 new promoted projects (with a total capital of 7.7 billion baht, employing 19,000 workers) were approved as compared to only 9 projects in the previous year. The investments appear to be centred in Songkhla, Yala, Klang, and Satun, and are mostly agro-industrial in nature. Examples include fruit processing, cold storage, aquaculture, downstream rubber products, marine products, and palm oil processing. Most of these projects have been assumed by Thai investors but several projects are reportedly joint ventures with Malaysian companies.

Light manufacturing activities in southern Thailand (especially those oriented to the export market) are hampered by higher labour cost, lack of critical skills, and poor infrastructure and transport links. Labour cost in southern Thailand is 50% higher than in the north-east. Here there is very little employable surplus labour as compared to the north-east. Combined with infrastructure deficiencies and lack of direct export transport linkages, labour-intensive light manufacturing operations are relocating from the metropolitan Bangkok area to the north-east, and increasingly to Lao PDR and Vietnam where wages are a fraction of those in Thailand. There may be greater scope for increased investment by Malaysian firms in various fruit and vegetable processing and downstream rubber products in southern Thailand. Compared to Malaysia, southern Thailand has relatively low-cost agricultural land, low-cost available labour and a well-developed technological edge in marine products and aquaculture (Stuyt and Honnald, 1994).

Northern Malaysia, particularly Penang, has been a magnet for foreign direct investment in export-oriented light manufacturing for the past three decades. Much of that investment has been in electronic components design and assembly located within free trade zones (see Table 2-5). Approximately 200 Malaysian companies supply components and undertake sub-contract work for the multinational companies (MNCs). The rapid industrialisation of Penang and the consequent labour shortage has already resulted in a considerable out-migration of labour-intensive industry to the more remote parts of northern Malaysia. Export-oriented garments assembly, for example, dominate industrial activity in Kedah and Perlis. Other industries have relocated to Vietnam and Indonesia. This outward movement of highly labour-intensive activities appears to have occurred in the absence of any specific government promotional policies or efforts (Salleh, 1994).

Inward investment in agricultural and agribusiness has slowed down due to escalating land prices, scarcity of agricultural land and the lack of unskilled labour. Malaysian companies engaged in estate crop cultivation (rubber, palm oil, cocoa and coconut) have been exporting their technology and investment to southern Thailand and Indonesia. Thai companies have invested in aquaculture in northern Malaysia to some

TABLE 2-5
Profile of Industrial Estate/EPZs in the IMT-GT Sub-Regions

	No. of Industrial Estates	Ownership	Total Area (ha.)	Area Developed (ha.)	Area Available for Occupancy (ha.)	No. of Firms	Total Employment	Price of Developed Land (US$/m^2)
Northern Sumatra								
Kawasan	1	Public	160	148	12	57	12,000	$24.05
(Medan)	1	Private	650	None	650	None	None	$9.52
Lamnotma	1	Private	300	None	300	None	None	
Northern Malaysia								
Kedah	15	Mostly public	758	440	152	125	25,000	$2.21–$19.23
Perak	20	Mostly public	1,775	900	415	242	23,000	$14.61–$23.85
Perlis	2	Public	30	19	10	9	2,000	$13.45
Penang	9	Mostly public	1,024	997	418	324	85,000	$41.38–$51.75
Southern Thailand								
Narathiwat	1	Not operational	100	None	n/a	None	None	$24.70
Pattani	1	Public						
Songkhla	1	Not operational						

Source: Information complied by consultant and mission estimates; 1990 data is used for northern Malaysia.

degree as evidenced by a recent investment in tiger prawns by a Middle Eastern company using Thai technology.

The restructuring of Malaysian industry has been postponed somewhat through the large-scale importation of unskilled and semi-skilled labour from Indonesia, Myanmar, Thailand, and elsewhere. According to some estimates, over one million foreign workers are currently employed in Malaysia, both legally and illegally. Unskilled production and agricultural workers are needed in less developed parts of the country. Skilled workers and technicians are being imported from the Indian subcontinent to Penang. While this approach has the advantage of preserving the competitiveness of Malaysian industry, it delays the restructuring of industry into more efficient means of production and deters movement of less competitive (labour-intensive) enterprises to labour surplus locations.

The pace of direct foreign inward investment in Indonesia as a whole has been slowing down over the past few years and has been declining in absolute terms over the past year. Although this in itself is not significant, it has resulted in the liberalisation of foreign investment regulations by the government of Indonesia in October 1993. Further liberalisation, including the easing of foreign-to-domestic equity transfer mandates, is imminent due to increasing pressure on the government and continuing declines in direct foreign investment.

Northern Sumatra and Aceh have not been major recipients of foreign or local direct investment as compared to other locations in Indonesia. Investment in northern Sumatra is increasing, particularly in Medan. The industrial estate in Medan is currently being expanded to accommodate new industrial activity. Several joint ventures reportedly have been established with Malaysian companies in textile manufacturing and other proposals have been made in various agribusiness and resource-based activities. Thai companies are said to be exploring investments in fishery activities (Wirkus, 1994).

In general, then, it appears that there are significant flows of investment, labour, and goods across the borders of Indonesia, Malaysia, and Thailand within the growth triangle area, even under conditions of significant constraints. We can conclude that these flows could be increased, formalised, and developed to the benefit of the people of all three countries if the constraints are eliminated in a systematic manner.

CONSTRAINTS TO THE DEVELOPMENT OF IMT-GT

Though the economies in the growth triangle region are growing at a fairly healthy pace among the sub-regions, these economies are not growing as fast as they could be because of certain constraints to profitable private sector production. Not surprisingly, they tend to vary by industry and region.

In terms of specific industrial investment possibilities, there is hope for labour-intensive enterprises to relocate to the Thai and Indonesian parts of the growth triangle but this is likely to vary significantly by industry. Agro-related industries and processes may be more likely to make cross-border investments as compared to electronics components manufacturers. While agro-related activities can benefit from the strong comparative advantages offered by resource-based activities in southern Thailand and northern Sumatra, more technologically advanced electronics manufacturers are deterred by numerous factors. These include:

(i) lack of an appropriately trained workforce;
(ii) poor industrial and transport infrastructure; and
(iii) lack of efficient transport services and linkages.

These factors may result in lower labour productivity and may also reduce cost competitiveness. Also, there may be no compelling economic reason to relocate operations to the border area given the existence of low labour-cost locations in the People's Republic of China, Vietnam and India, and the alternative possibility of greater automation.

The potential for Penang to develop into the logistics and services hub for the sub-region is significant but this will depend on the extent to which neighbouring governments will allow the free flow of goods across borders and the rational utilisation of transport facilities and infrastructure. Successful restructuring of the economy will depend on the ability to upgrade manpower to provide a skilled and technical workforce necessary for more capital-intensive activity.

While there are possible investment complementarities among all three areas in the IMT-GT, the investment potential of the northern Sumatra/Aceh part of the growth triangle is constrained by several factors. The major constraints include:

(i) concerns over transparency and speed of investment approvals process (the approval is said to be long and cumbersome and exacerbated by differences in national local policies);
(ii) lack of adequately trained labour in northern Sumatra;
(iii) various "informal" barriers to foreign investment, including the presence of monopolies which impede access to the domestic Indonesian market; and
(iv) limits on foreign ownership of land-based activities and mandatory divestment requirements for promoted companies.

In addition to these country-specific constraints, several conditions seem to apply to all three sub-regions. Some of the more obvious constraints are:

(i) general national-level trade policies, including cumbersome customs procedures, high tariffs, quotas, and price controls;
(ii) sub-optimal labour policies, including lack of training and cumbersome and ineffective constraints on labour movement;
(iii) conflicting investment policies, including differing and onerous constraints on foreign ownership, restrictions on land use by foreigners, constraints on access to local markets and financial restrictions;
(iv) lack of information on potential sites and partners for joint investment in the sub-regions;
(v) capital constraints on small local joint venture partners as well as broad financial restraints on foreign investment;
(vi) poor technical extension and support services with little international cooperation, especially in the field of agriculture; and
(vii) visa, licensing, and travel restrictions between the three countries, including restrictions on individual and vehicular transportation across borders, difficulties of customs clearance and general bureaucratic road blocking.

OPPORTUNITIES OF GROWTH FOR PENANG

Compared to the other parts of the IMT-GT, Penang already had an established industrial base in the early eighties with manufacturing comprising 40% of GDP. The tourism, services, energy, transportation and communication industries are also advanced in the Penang area. On the other hand, there is an overall shortage of technical, skilled and unskilled labour force in Penang. This may undermine not only the process of further development but, also, prevent Penang from attaining high technology oriented industrial development and from achieving high-value added industry.

The formation of the IMT-GT will provide tremendous opportunities for Penang's economy. Since the other regions in the IMT-GT are better endowed with labour, labour-intensive companies from Penang could be relocated there. The industrial sector of northern Sumatra and south Thailand will be achieved through the provision of industrial estates and labour while technical and managerial expertise, as well as capital, would be provided by Penang. Penang, on the other hand, should develop the more technical and skill intensive and higher value-added industry. The industrial base should be diversified. Other possible areas of cooperation which may benefit Penang include the following:

(i) Given the trend of air traffic growth between Kuala Lumpur/Penang, there is potential for a joint service between MAS and Garuda similar to that between Penang and Thailand.
(ii) With the healthy increase in traffic between Belawan Port and Penang Port, the establishment of a link between the two ports would help to facilitate port trade as Penang is already linked to Singapore and this would enhance trade between these two ports.
(iii) There is tremendous potential for freight forwarders in the Thai/Malaysian border trade. With the formation of the Thai Cargo Committee to attract and streamline Thai trade through Penang Port as well as the establishment of the Padang Besar by 1993, container traffic is expected to increase above the current average of 1,400 TEUs a month. It may be necessary to secure some form of Thai government participation in ensuring that the border trade through Penang Port is not disrupted.
(iv) Currently, there are discussions which have been initiated by Telekoms Malaysia on common standards for maritime communication in the ASEAN region. The International Maritime Service operated by Telekoms Malaysia is currently unprofitable due to insufficient traffic. With Penang as a regional hub for shipping, there is potential for making this a profitable venture.

(v) Private sector interaction relations between the respective Chambers of Commerce should be fostered on a trilateral basis. This would improve the bargaining positions for joint purchase and sale, the sharing of market information and technical expertise, and establishing sub-contracting activities.

(vi) Technology and technical cooperation may lead to the sub-contracting of production processes, taking into consideration factor endowments and prices. The northern peninsular component in general, and Penang in particular, could also take the lead in education and training to ensure the correct mix of skills.

CONCLUSION

Initial investigation has indicated fairly clearly that developments in the IMT-GT are desirable and feasible. It is supported by the existence of complementarities in terms of inputs and products among the sub-regions. The IMT-GT will help the participating countries maintain their global export competitiveness through regional cooperation and derive efficiency gains from lower transportation, labour and raw material costs. The triangle will also increase social welfare as a result of increased sub-regional flows of goods, services and labour.

But it should be emphasised also that the realisation of the benefit of the IMT-GT will require great efforts. The three participating national and local governments should realise the consequent requirement for some degree of policy reforms and project finance, and fully commit themselves to support the objectives of greater inter-regional trade and investment. The growth triangle also requires the simplification of administrative procedures and the elimination of bureaucratic hindrances. A successful growth triangle needs an optimal mix of public sector actions and policies, and private sector initiatives, since neither can sustain the implementation of the triangle by themselves.

REFERENCES

Chen Edward K. Y. and Anne Ho, "Southern China Growth Triangle: An Overview", in *Growth Triangle in Asia: A New Approach to*

Regional Economic Cooperation, edited by M. Thant and M. Tang. Oxford University Press, 1994.

Chia Siew Yue and Lee Tsao-Yuan, "Sub-regional Economic Zones: A New Motive Force in Asia-Pacific Development". Paper presented at the 20th Pacific Trade and Development Conference, Washington, DC, September 1992.

Lall Sanjaya, "Study on Industry and Energy Sector of Indonesia-Malaysia-Thailand Growth Triangle, Mid-Term Report". Manila, Philippines, April 1994.

Naseem Syed M., "IMT-GT Development-Overview", in *Indonesia-Malaysia-Thailand Growth Triangle Development*, edited by M. Thant and M. Tang. Asian Development Bank, June 1994.

Rao Kishore, "Study on Trade, Investment and Labour Mobility of Indonesia-Malaysia-Thailand Growth Triangle, Mid-Term Report". Manila, Philippines, April 1994.

Salleh Ismail bin Muhd, "IMT-GT Development-Malaysia", in *Indonesia-Malaysia-Thailand Growth Triangle Development*, edited by M. Thant and M. Tang. Asian Development Bank, June 1994.

Stuyt Johan C. and Michael J. Honnald, "IMT-GT Development-Thailand", in *Indonesia-Malaysia-Thailand Growth Triangle Development*, edited by M. Thant and M. Tang. Asian Development Bank, June 1994.

Summer Lawrence H., "Regionalisalism and the World Trade System". Paper presented at the Federal Reserve Bank of Kansas City, August 1991.

Tang Min and Myo Thant, "Growth Triangles: Conceptual Issues and Operational Problems", in *Growth Triangle in Asia: A New Approach to Regional Economic Cooperation*, edited by M. Thant and M. Tang. Oxford University Press, 1994.

Thant Myo and Min Tang, "Growth Triangles: Fad or Fact", in *Indonesia-Malaysia-Thailand Growth Triangle Development*, edited by M. Thant and M. Tang. Asian Development Bank, June 1994.

Wirkus Winifred Lydya, "IMT-GT Development-Indonesia", in *Indonesia-Malaysia-Thailand Growth Triangle Development*, edited by M. Thant and M. Tang. Asian Development Bank, June 1994.

Chapter 3

The Penang Economy

BY
Lilian NG Mui Hoon
Kristie YEONG Chia Huey

INTRODUCTION

PENANG IS THE second smallest state of Peninsular Malaysia in terms of land area, comprising approximately 1,031 sq. km. It consists of the island of Penang which comprises only 293 sq. km; and the Wellesley Province situated on the north-western coast of mainland Malaysia (bounded to the north and east by the State of Kedah and to the south by the State of Perak) which comprises the remaining 738 sq. km.

The British were probably the first to recognise the strategic position of Penang as an important trading centre in the Straits of Malacca and Sumatra. Penang's port served not only the northern part of west Malaysia, north Sumatra and south Thailand but also Myanmar and India. However, its role as a trading centre was significantly reduced when Penang lost its free port status in the 1960s. As a result, Penang's economy faltered.

And yet, today, Penang is one of the fastest growing economies in Malaysia. It is recognised as an industrialised state. In 1991, for instance, Penang's gross domestic product (GDP) grew by 11%. Between now and the year 2000, Penang is expected to achieve an average annual growth rate of at least 7%.[1]

---

[1] *Penang into the 21st Century*, an official publication of the Penang State Government, October 1992.

Penang has a stable socio-political environment and a steadily growing economy. In addition, the Penang State Government is responsive to business needs and has identified the necessary strategies to develop Penang into a business centre.

THE PENANG ECONOMY

Penang's prosperity can be attributed mainly to its success in attracting foreign investments into the manufacturing sector which now accounts for about one-half of the state's GDP. The dominant industries are the electrical and electronic sub-sectors which account for about 36% of total manufacturing employment.

However, with the liberalisation of the economies of Indochina and China, along with the rapid economic development of the other ASEAN countries in the region, the competition for foreign investment funds will increase. Furthermore, Penang's traditional investors also are facing domestic economic difficulties and they will have limited funds for overseas investments. Besides, Penang has to contend with competition from the other Malaysian states which may also be interested in pursuing an industrialisation agenda. Penang, therefore, faces a very serious threat of investment diversion. Already the foreign capital investment in the state has shrunk from a peak of RM1,489 million in 1990 to RM236 million in 1993.[2]

To cope with this trend, one strategy is for Penang to diversify its economy by promoting "higher-order services" through emphasising the development of the business and service sectors. It is interesting to note that currently, Penang's tertiary sector accounts for 47% of the state's GDP. However, the share of the finance, insurance, real estate and business service sectors has been maintained only at about 9% over the two decades from 1970 to 1990, and this has been due mainly to a robust real estate sub-sector.[3] A summary of these sectors and their contributions to Penang's GDP is presented in Table 3-1.

In an interview with the *Singapore Straits Times* in April 1993, the Chief Minister of Penang, Dr. Koh Tsu Koon, expressed his wish to

---

2 Manmohan Singh, "Foreign Direct Investment in Penang", a paper presented at the NTU MBA Business Mission to Penang, February 1994.

3 *Penang into the 21st Century*, an official publication of the Penang State Government, October 1992.

develop Penang into an "economic powerhouse by the year 2020". One of his plans is to make Penang "a regional financial and commercial hub".[4]

TABLE 3-1
Penang's Gross Domestic Product (in 1978 constant prices)

Sector	1970 RM (m)	%	1980 RM (m)	%	1990 RM (m)	%
Primary						
Agriculture, Livestock, Forestry & Fishing	264	19.5	223	6.5	189	3.3
Mining & Quarrying	2	0.2	18	0.5	26	0.5
Secondary						
Manufacturing	172	12.7	1,399	41.0	2,668	46.0
Construction	78	5.8	143	4.2	170	2.9
Tertiary						
Electricity, Gas & Water	42	3.1	68	2.0	116	2.0
Transport, Storage & Communications	101	7.5	313	9.2	648	11.2
Wholesale & Retail Trade, Hotels & Restaurants						
Finance, Insurance, Real Estate & Business Services	361	26.7	565	16.6	731	12.6
Government Services	131	9.7	269	7.9	540	9.3
Other Services	58	4.3	322	9.4	563	9.7
	142	10.5	93	2.7	143	2.5
Total	1,351	100.0	3,413	100.0	5,794	100.0

Source: *Penang into the 21st Century*, an official publication of the Penang State Government, October 1991.

PENANG AS A BUSINESS CENTRE

A study of existing business centres reveals that certain basic requirements, comprising multidimensional considerations, must be in place before a business centre can be successful. These requirements include the following:

---

4 *The Straits Times*, 17 April 1993.

(i) A high quality, competent and productive workforce which is knowledgeable in matters of trade and commerce.
(ii) A good economic environment including favourable regulatory systems, stable currency, low inflation rate, minimum restrictions on exchange control, attractive taxation policies, etc.
(iii) Sound infrastructure facilities, including an efficient telecommunications and postal network, complemented by adequate physical infrastructure such as sea, air, rail and road transportation facilities, and reliable supplies of public utilities (electricity, gas and water).
(iv) Government support, including investment incentives, which encourages the development of commerce and trading activities.
(v) Political stability and capable administrative leadership.
(vi) Social, racial and cultural harmony.

Although Penang has the basic requirements to become a business centre, it will face a number of challenges in achieving its objectives. Several of the more important ones are discussed below.

Domestic Perspective

First, and foremost, the development of Penang as a regional business centre must be within the national objectives set by the federal government, and it must fit into the overall national development plan. For instance, it would not be in the interest of the country for the effect of any development in Penang to detract from Kuala Lumpur's role as the country's premier business centre. One possibility is to position Penang to serve mainly the northern states of Peninsular Malaysia, that is, Perlis, Perak and Kedah. However, considering the proximity of Penang and Kuala Lumpur, one wonders if there is a real need to establish two separate business centres. It is worth noting that many of the investment incentives and taxation policies that Penang has to offer are co-ordinated by the federal government. The support of the federal government is crucial if Penang is to succeed as a regional business centre.

Potential in the IMT-GT

Apart from the domestic scene, the proposed Indonesia-Malaysia-Thailand Growth Triangle (IMT-GT) provides an exciting opportunity for Penang to use its comparative advantage. The proposed growth triangle comprises the two Indonesian provinces of northern Sumatra and Aceh, the four northern Malaysian states of Perlis, Kedah, Penang and Perak, and the five southern Thai provinces of Satun, Yala, Narathiwat, Pattani and Songkhla. Of all the partners in the economic group, Penang is the most industrialised and its service, energy, transportation and communication industries are the most developed. This makes Penang suitable to assume the role of a business centre for the region. However, whether Penang will be successful in playing this role depends on the extent to which the neighbouring governments allow it to do so. For instance, from the viewpoints of Indonesia and Thailand, it would be more desirable to develop a business centre of their own such as Medan in Indonesia and Haadyai in Thailand.

Fundamentally, the success of the IMT-GT concept depends on recognising economic complementarity and requires political commitment on the part of all its partners. At the moment, issues concerning the harmonisation of infrastructure and institutional frameworks (such as employment regulations and tariff policies, etc.) still need to be resolved.

The future of the IMT-GT is also uncertain. Unlike the southern China Growth Triangle and the Johor-Singapore-Riau Growth Triangle which have Hong Kong and Singapore as their respective locomotives, the IMT-GT does not yet have a strong enough locomotive to ensure the success of the grouping. However, we are of the view that Penang can position itself as the locomotive since it possesses the expertise, experience and economic prowess compared to other partners in the IMT-GT.

Globalisation Trend

In the past, locational factors, such as accessibility in time zone or geography, were sources of competitive advantage in the development of a regional business centre. However, with the advent of technology (i.e., computers, satellites and electronic banking networks) the constraints of time zone or geography have almost been eliminated. Business can be conducted anytime and anywhere. Penang's location in the Straits of Malacca is not enough to guarantee its success as a business centre for the region. Having said this, however, it must be acknowledged that in the current uncertain global economic environment, Asia is the world's fastest developing region and the growth in intra-Asian trade augurs well for Penang. Competition will be tough but it is not a zero sum game. Penang's future depends on the development of the Malaysian economy as well as the overall progress of IMT-GT.

PENANG'S HUMAN RESOURCE SITUATION

Penang's workforce is predominantly young (the median age for males is 30 and for females it is 29), is well-educated (about 60% have attained secondary education), and is skilled (about 9% of the labour force comprises professional, technical, administrative and managerial workers, and around 25% are employed as clerical and sales workers). Tables 3-2, 3-3, 3-4 and 3-5, give a more comprehensive breakdown of these factors. The English language is widely used as the medium of business transactions.

TABLE 3-2
Principal Statistics on Penang's Labour Force: 1990

Total Working Age Group (15–64)	
Labour Force	469,000
Labour Force Participation Rate	63.4%
Male Labour Force Participation Rate	86.0%
Female Labour Force Participation Rate	44.5%
Total Employed	446,000
Total Unemployed	23,000 (4.9%)

Source: Ismail bin Muhd. Salleh, Institute of Strategic and International Studies, "Indonesia-Malaysia-Thailand Growth Triangle Development Project" Inception Meeting Report, 1993.

PENANG'S INFRASTRUCTURE FRAMEWORK

Communications Facilities

Penang has adequate telecommunications and postal services to meet current needs. For instance, the state has a telephone penetration of 14 telephones per 100 population which is higher than the national average of 10.[5] Postal services in Penang, as in the rest of Malaysia, are the responsibility of the newly privatised Pos Malaysia while Telekom

---

5 *Investment in Penang Malaysia*, an official publication of the Penang Development Corporation, 1993.

Malaysia is responsible for all telegraph and public telephone services. The services available include a nationwide telephone service with subscribers trunk dialing (STD), international subscriber dialing services (ISD), car-phone service, mobile radio telephone service, radio paging service, toll free service, high frequency radio call service, radio maritime service and leased channel radio telephone service. Telekom Malaysia also has a video-conferencing studio in Penang which offers communication with studios in Kuala Lumpur, Kuching, Johor Bahru and Kuantan as well as with studios in other countries via satellite.

TABLE 3-3
Working-age Population: 1980–1991

	1980		1991	
Age Group	**Number**	**Percentage**	**Number**	**Percentage**
0–14	307,163	34.1	324,848	30.5
15–64	554,876	61.6	689,103	64.7
> 64	38,733	4.3	51,124	4.8
Total	900,772	100.0	1,065,075	100.0
Dependency Ratio		0.62		0.55

Source: *Statistics, Penang Malaysia*, official publication by Penang Development Corporation, 1993.

TABLE 3-4
Level of Education of Employed Persons: 1989

Source	**Percentage**
College/University	4.1
Secondary	60.1
Primary	31.4
No Formal Education	4.2

Source: *Statistics, Penang Malaysia*, official publication by Penang Development Corporation, 1993.

TABLE 3-5
Percentage Distribution of Employed Persons by Occupational Groups: 1989

Group	Percentage
Professional, Technical & Related Workers	6.5
Administrative & Managerial Workers	2.3
Clerical & Related Workers	11.5
Sales & Related Workers	13.2
Service Workers	13.3
Agriculture, Animal Husbandry & Forestry, Fisherman & Hunters	7.2
Production, Transport Equipment Operators & Labourers	46.0

Source: *Statistics, Penang Malaysia*, official publication by Penang Development Corporation, 1993.

Port Facilities

Penang's deep-water harbour is the second largest port in the country. In 1992, the port handled 13 million tonnes of cargo. In recent years, the Penang Port Commission has embarked on a number of development projects to expand and modernise the existing port facilities to cater for the rapid increase in cargo handled by the Port. One of the development projects is the construction of the north Butterworth Container Terminal (NBCT) which was completed in late 1994. The new terminal, together with the present Butterworth Container Terminal, will provide a total combined capacity of 482,500 TEUs which will sustain projected growth until the year 2000.[6]

Air Facilities

Located on Penang Island, the Bayan Lepas International Airport is one of six international airports in Malaysia. In terms of service area and traffic volume, the Bayan Lepas Airport ranks second after the Subang Airport in Kuala Lumpur. It is the main line terminus for the Malaysia Airlines (MAS) West Coast domestic route and it has direct services to Singapore, Bangkok, Medan, Haadyai, Madras, Taipei and Hong Kong. In 1989, passenger traffic handled by the airport was 1.52 million and

---

[6] Source: Penang Development Corporation.

cargo traffic was 22,600 tonnes. Recently, the airport was upgraded with a new Air Cargo Complex.[7]

Railway Facilities

Rail service for the State of Penang is provided by the newly incorporated KTM Berhad. Along with Singapore, Kuala Lumpur and Ipoh, Butterworth in Wellesley Province is a principal rail terminus of the Peninsular Malaysia rail network. KTM also provides both freight and passenger services between Butterworth, the States of Kedah, Perak and southern Thailand. With its incorporation, KTM has undertaken to increase the transportation capacity, improve reliability, and enhance the quality and scope of services. Currently, the Butterworth-Prai freight terminal handles approximately 400,000 tonnes of cargo per year.[8]

Road Transportation Facilities

The road network is relatively well-developed in Penang and it has a road length/area ratio of 2.11.[9] However, current traffic bottlenecks occur along certain segments of the Federal Route 1, such as the Butterworth-Taiping stretch between Kulim and Butterworth, and in the urban areas of Penang Island as well as Butterworth and Bukit Mertajam. The traffic congestion on Federal Route 1 has been resolved with the opening of the entire north-south expressway link between Bukit Kayu Hitam and Ipoh and the east-west highway.

Electric Power Supply

In Penang, electric power is supplied by the Tenaga Nasional Berhad (TNB). In the past few years, Penang has had a problem of electricity shortage. This problem will be even more serious in the future. The projected demand for power supply in the year 2000 is 1240 mega-watts which is almost double the existing plant capacities.[10] Efforts have been taken by TNB to upgrade five power stations at Klang, Selangor, Johor, Perak and Malacca to generate an additional 517 mega-watts.

---

7 Source: Penang Development Corporation.

8 Source: Penang Development Corporation.

9 *Investment in Penang Malaysia*, an official publication of Penang Development Corporation, 1993.

10 Salleh Ismail bin Muhd., "Indonesia-Malaysia-Thailand Growth Triangle Development Project", Inception Meeting Report, 1993.

Water Supply

The water supply within the State of Penang is managed by the Penang Water Authority. On Penang Island, the water from six rivers and adjacent streams provides a direct supply to three treatment plants while Wellesley Province has five separate sources of water supply. The water systems on the island and the mainland are connected by two submarine pipelines across the channel. This enables the mainland to supply the island with water and vice-versa. The existing capacity of water supply is adequate to meet the present demand of the state which is about 523 million litres per day,[11] inclusive of both domestic and industrial demand.

CONCLUSION

Penang's economy is dominated overwhelmingly by the manufacturing industry, particularly the electrical and electronic sectors, nearly all of which are supported by foreign investments. The ability to sustain and improve on the level of foreign investments into Penang is crucial, therefore, to the state's economic progress.

The development of Penang into a regional business centre has potential because Penang possesses the "critical success factors" necessary to achieve the objective. In the final analysis, however, it is the regionalised growth-oriented macro policies, sound human resource management and firm political commitment from all parties concerned that holds the key to Penang's development as a regional business centre.

---

11 *Investment in Penang Malaysia*, an official publication of Penang Development Corporation.

FORMS OF BUSINESS AND INCENTIVES

Chapter 4

Joint Ventures and Partnerships: Critical Success Factors

BY
Sally ONG Kar Imm
TAN Siok Leng

INTRODUCTION

FOREIGN INVESTORS HAVE been an important impetus to the robust economic growth in Penang in recent years. Attracted by its strategic location, well-developed supporting industries, well-disciplined and competitive workforce, Penang has been one of the favoured locations of investors for manufacturing projects in Malaysia. To-date, apart from companies from the Asia Pacific region, Penang also hosts international MNCs such as Motorola, Hewlett-Packard (HP), Sony, etc. The presence of MNCs in Penang also enhances the development pace of Penang's local industries.

Given the importance of foreign investments to Penang's economic development, this report critically evaluates the factors that lure foreign investors to Penang. It will also review factors that may potentially contribute to a fruitful and successful business venture in Penang, Malaysia.

FOREIGN INVESTMENTS IN PENANG

Spearheaded by the rapid growth of its

manufacturing sector, Penang recorded a GDP growth rate of 11% in 1991 and it is expected to achieve an average growth rate of at least 7% until the year 2000.[1]

Of the 83 projects approved in Penang in 1993, 35 were for the manufacture of electrical and electronic products, and 13 were for plastic products. The breakdown of companies by type of industry (see Table 4-1) highlights the concentration in the electrical and electronics industry which employed about 89,402 workers at the end of June 1993, or slightly more than one-half of the total workforce in Penang.

TABLE 4-1
Distribution of Workers by Industry

Type of Industry	No. of Factors	No. of Workers
Electronics/Electrical	142	89,402
Fabricated Metal	107	11,078
Plastics	62	6,678
Chemical/Fertiliser	47	3,569
Paper/Printing	43	4,272
Textiles/Garments	26	13,028

Source: *Statistics, Penang Malaysia*, official publication by Penang Development Corporation.

In line with investment trends across Malaysia, proposed total foreign capital investment has dropped from a peak of RM1.5 billion in 1990 to RM236 million in 1993. However, small and medium sized local companies have grown, and they are poised to assume a greater role in the future development of Penang. This is evidenced by the increase in proposed local investments which, in 1993, accounted for about 55% of the proposed total capital investment. This surpasses proposed foreign investments for the first time since 1987.[2]

---

1 *Penang into the 21st Century*, an official publication of the Penang State Government, October 1992.

2 Manmohan Singh, "Foreign Investment in Penang", a paper presented at the NTU MBA Business Mission to Penang, February 1994.

RATIONALE AND INCENTIVES TO INVEST IN PENANG

Foreign investors have been attracted to Penang for several reasons. Some of the more significant ones are described briefly in the following sub-sections.

Strategic Location

With its developed infrastructure and telecommunication systems, Penang is strategically located with easy access to the outside world. The proposed IMT-GT will further enhance Penang's position as a favoured location for other MNCs that wish to expand their business to this region.

Cost Advantage

While wages in Penang have been on a rising trend, they remain relatively competitive as compared to Singapore. According to the latest industrial survey, the median starting wage rate for skilled production workers ranges from RM12.50 to RM 17.40 per day while for unskilled production workers, wages range from RM8.60 to RM11.30 per day. This labour cost advantage, coupled with the low cost of living and low inflation rate, translates into great savings for companies.

Political/Economic Stability

Penang has enjoyed political stability over the last few decades. The Penang State Government has always been supportive of the industrialisation of Penang. It has offered a wide range of tax incentives and facilities to investors in its bid to actively promote investment in the manufacturing sector.

Good Investment Climate

The Penang government provides a comprehensive range of incentives to attract foreign investors. Some of the more important incentives include the following:

(i) ***Pioneer Status:*** Companies given pioneer status only have to pay tax on 30% of their statutory income for a period of five years. Tax relief of 100% may be granted for strategic projects of national importance.
(ii) ***Investment Tax Allowances:*** An allowance of 60% related to capital

expenditures incurred within five years will be granted. The allowance can be used to offset 70% of the statutory income; however, the balance of 30% will be taxed at the prevailing company tax rate.

(iii) ***Reinvestment Allowance:*** The reinvestment allowance is in the form of an allowance of 50% of capital expenditures incurred by a company in the expansion of production capacity, modernisation and upgrading of production facilities, and diversification into related products. Since the beginning of January 1996, the allowance has been extended to agricultural projects.

(iv) ***General Incentives:*** There are many incentives provided by the Malaysian government to promote specific objectives such as export, research and development, training, storage/treatment/disposal of toxic and hazardous waste, etc. To encourage companies to look beyond Malaysia, and to expand their geographical coverage worldwide by exporting their products, there are many incentives for exports such as the export credit refinancing scheme, double deduction of export credit insurance premiums, double deduction for promotion of exports, and industrial building allowances.

Apart from these incentives, a distinctive feature that makes Penang an attractive place for investors, is the professionally operated Penang Development Corporation (PDC). The PDC offers a wide range of services to assist investors, such as liaising with the state and federal agencies on facilities that may be required by investors. It is interesting to note that while Singapore has many specialised agencies to handle specific functions, such as the Housing and Development Board to take care of housing development and the Economic Development Board to concentrate on industrial development, in Penang, all of these functions are undertaken by the PDC and it has proven to be very effective and efficient. PDC's main activities include the following:

(a) Industrial Development and Promotion;
(b) Housing and New Township Development;
(c) Urban Redevelopment;
(d) Tourism Promotion; and
(e) Land Reclamation and Development.

Good Infrastructure

To encourage foreign investments, the PDC introduced the concept of Free Trade Zones (FTZs) for export-oriented activities. To date, it has seven free industrial zones and five industrial parks. The FTZs are well-equipped with the necessary facilities to handle business operations and they are offered at very attractive rates. In addition, the industrial parks are all strategically located near the port, airport and railway station, and thus are linked by an efficient network of transportation.

Penang's infrastructure is adequate for its current needs although further improvements can be expected as the economy develops. Penang has good easy access to all the major cities of the world. It has direct air links with the Asian countries and, via Kuala Lumpur, links to all the major cities in the world. In addition, the telecommunications and postal facilities also enable easy access to various parts of the world.

Quality of Life

The cost of living is low in Penang. Housing is affordable and a wide variety of delicious local foods can be had at reasonable prices. People enjoy a pleasant pace of life with sandy beaches on the north coast which offers excellent facilities for sunbathing, swimming, boating and other sea sports. In addition, medical, health, shopping and education facilities are easily available. It should be noted that Penang has several international schools that cater for the children of expatriates. An important factor that makes Penang a pleasant place to stay is the friendliness of its people.

Good Disciplined Workforce

Just like Singapore, most of the workforce are easily "trainable" since most of them have some basic education. While this factor may hold in many countries, Penang has an added advantage in that its workforce is highly disciplined.

Good Supporting Industries

The presence of good supporting industries is an important factor that gives Penang a competitive edge over other states. It is also a factor that lures international MNCs to Penang.

FOREIGN INVESTMENT GUIDELINES AND PROTECTION

While encouraging foreign investment, the Government of Malaysia also places much emphasis on the development of local industries. As such, it strongly encourages projects to be undertaken on a joint venture basis to ensure that the objective of increasing Malaysian participation in manufacturing activities is attained.

Following the relaxation of the Bumiputra Ruling, foreign investors now have greater flexibility in terms of equity ownership in Malaysia. As summarised in Table 4-2, the extent of equity ownership will depend on the export ratio of a company.

TABLE 4-2
Guidelines on Equity Ownership

% of Export to Total Production	Limit on Foreign Equity Ownership
> 80%	100%
50% < X < 80%	51% – 79%
20% < X < 50%	30% – 51%
< 20%	30% (max)

Source: *Policies and Incentives, Penang Malaysia*, an official publication of Penang Development Corporation, 1993.

For projects that export 50% or more, but less than 80% of their production, foreign equity ownership of up to 100% can be allowed if the following conditions are met:

(i) Foreign investments exceed RM50 million in fixed assets (excluding land);
(ii) Projects which have at least 50% value added are implemented; and
(iii) A company's products do not compete with local domestic products.

In cases where foreign equity is less than 100%, the balance of equity will be distributed in accordance with the guidelines shown in Table 4-3.

For example, if a foreign company owns 60% of the equity, 30% will be reserved for bumiputras; the balance will go to non-bumiputras. Although the allocation seems to favour bumiputras, in cases where equity reserved for is not taken up, MITI will allocate the balance to non-bumiputras.

For the Singaporean venturing to Penang, networking can even start at the undergraduate or MBA level with student counterparts from Malaysia. These sources can pave the way to building and fostering good business relationships because the resident Malaysians are acquainted with the culture, the style of doing business, and the market in Malaysia. They can be hired as potential managers for joint ventures and their understanding of the country will help to eradicate unnecessary "initial start-up" preparatory work.

TABLE 4-3
Guidelines on Distribution of Foreign Equity Ownership

Type of Joint Venture	Foreign Equity > 70%	Foreign Equity < 70%
Between 2 Foreigners	Balance: Bumiputras	30%: Bumiputras Balance: Non-bumiputras
Between 1 Foreigner and 1 Bumiputra	Balance: Bumiputras	Balance: Bumiputras
Between 1 Foreigner and 1 Non-bumiputra	Balance: Non-bumiputras	30%: Non-bumiputras Balance: Bumiputras

Source: *Policies and Incentives, Penang Malaysia,* an official publication of Penang Development Corporation, 1993.

Partnership Management

A Singapore company intending to establish joint ventures in Penang may do so using one of the following three forms:

(a) Joint Venture with MNC;
(b) Joint Venture with Bumiputra company/investor; or
(c) Joint Venture with Non-bumiputra company/investor.

For a small company, starting a joint venture with an MNC is only a remote possibility. According to informed sources, and following the relaxation of the Bumiputra ruling, most MNCs in Penang would prefer to have a 100% equity stake. This would provide them with better control. Moreover, foreign MNCs would prefer local partners with more intimate information on the local operating environment.

In our opinion, joint ventures with bumiputra or non-bumiputra companies in the support industries will provide better opportunities for small investors. The biggest challenge is to find a trustworthy local partner. For investors who are new to Penang or Malaysia, one short cut is to enlist the help of PDC. An investor should also be sensitive to the environment in which the business operates.

Identifying Realisable Opportunities

Investors looking for growth opportunities in Penang should be cognisant of Penang's stage of economic development and the shift in its focus as the economy matures. Having been very successful in attracting big players such as Sony, HP, Motorola, etc, Penang is now working towards building up domestically-led manufacturing capacity, and progressively shifting to higher technology industries which are more capital-intensive and which possess the following characteristics:

(a) High value-added;
(b) Capital-intensive;
(c) Skill-intensive;
(d) Non-polluting; and
(e) Non-labour intensive and able to provide forward and backward linkages.

When investing in Penang, investors have to keep in mind all of these characteristics. A visionary company that can offer these strengths will blend in well with Penang's state of economic development, and will generate activities mutually beneficial to both parties.

Understanding of Social/Culture/Region Environment in Penang

While English is widely used in Penang, knowledge of Bahasa Malaysia will help in improving communications with workers. An investor should understand the different pace of work among the workers. Religion plays a major role in guiding the ethical behaviour of workers in the workplace. For example, Muslim workers may leave for prayers after lunch. Provision of prayer rooms will motivate and encourage worker loyalty. During the fasting month, employers need to be more understanding, particularly to blue collar workers whose work is more physically strenuous.

Training/Retention of Workforce

As Penang moves towards high-technology industrialisation, the need for training will become more apparent. To cut training costs, companies should take advantage of courses and facilities offered by various training centres in Penang. Synergistically, this will work towards a better trained workforce. The Penang Skills Development Centre is one organisation which provides application-based training for the workforce.

Given the tight labour situation in Penang, one of the main concerns of management is to retain good workers. The challenge is to devise new employee retention benefits aimed at instilling greater loyalty to the firm.

CONCLUSION

The latest pragmatic approach to foreign-local equity ownership rulings certainly has boosted the presence of foreign investors. Such policy relaxation is most timely and appropriate in view of the greater vigour it can bring to the market forces in the attraction of foreign direct investment.

Chapter 5

Tax System, Incentives and Compliance Reporting in Penang

BY
TAY Lim Hock
LEE Wah Seng
Sasi KUMAR
WONG Meng Ling

INTRODUCTION

IN MALAYSIA, THE federal government is the policy maker and the various states, including Penang, have very little say in deciding on the tax structure, business incentives and corporate reporting requirements. Therefore, the following discussions, although focused within the framework of Penang, will also apply to the whole of Malaysia.

CORPORATE AND PERSONAL TAXATION

General

The tax year is the calendar year ending 31 December and each tax year is referred to as the "Year of Assessment". As in Singapore, income is subject to tax on a preceding year basis. For example, income earned in the year 1993 will be taxed in the year of assessment which is 1994.

Scope

A company is either "resident" or "non-resident" for tax purposes depending on the location of its central management and its control. It is considered a resident if control and management of one or more of its operations is exercised in Malaysia. A company is subject to tax on income derived from Malaysia. Offshore income not received in Penang is not subject to tax in Penang.

Dividend income is taxable unless it is distributed out of tax exempt profits. Dividends received from other Malaysian corporations and some Singapore corporations, however, may carry a credit that eliminates the tax payable on the dividend.

Tax Rates

The current tax rate of corporate income is 27% and 30% for Singapore and Malaysia, respectively (with effect from the year of assessment, 1995). These rates apply to both resident and non-resident companies. Both Singapore and Malaysia have a significant number of tax relief mechanisms as investment incentives. These will be discussed in a subsequent section of this chapter.

A corporation's income tax is computed based on taxable income for the accounting year ending in the preceding calendar year. Income derived from non-business sources, (e.g., dividends, interest, rents and royalties) are assessed on the preceding calendar year basis.

Withholding Tax

There are three major categories subject to withholding tax:

(i) ***Royalties:*** Under a number of tax treaties, royalties can be totally exempt from the normal 27% rate of Singapore withholding tax. However, each treaty should be reviewed in detail as the exemptions are not all-embracing. In other cases, certain specified royalties can qualify for exemption, notwithstanding the reduced rates already provided for by tax treaty. The withholding tax rate on royalties payment for Malaysia is 15%. The definition of royalty is broad but does not extend to management fees unless the fees are for technical services.

(ii) ***Management Fees:*** The Singapore withholding tax can be negotiated downwards from 27% if the non-residents can demonstrate that these are costs incurred in deriving the fees. In Malaysia, these are referred to as "technical service payments" which are deemed to be derived from Malaysia, and they are subject to 10% withholding tax if paid to a non-resident. The rates may be reduced under certain treaties.

(iii) ***Capital Gains:*** Capital gains are generally not taxable in either Malaysia or Singapore except that, in the case of Malaysia, capital gains from the sale or disposal of land or any interest, options and rights in or over land situated in Malaysia, are subject to real property gains tax ranging from 5% to 30% effective from 27 October 1995 depending on the holding period of the land. Disposal of land under certain circumstances is exempt from real property gains tax.

Tax Losses

For both Malaysia and Singapore, business losses may generally be carried forward indefinitely and offset against future profits of the corporation. Losses of prior years may not be offset against non-business income. However, for Singapore, the criteria for the minimum 50% substantial beneficial ownership must be satisfied.

Capital allowances may be carried forward and offset only against adjusted income from the same business source which is not utilised. Therefore, if a company ceases operations, or changes its activities substantially, any unabsorbed capital allowances will be lost. Like Singapore, operating losses cannot be carried back against taxable income.

Capital Allowances

Capital allowances are given for expenditures incurred on the provision of plant and machinery used for the purpose of a business, industrial buildings, or capital expenditure incurred in connection with the working of a farm, plantation or forest. Buildings which are used for approved research and development, or industrial training, also qualify for industrial building allowances. This treatment is the same as Singapore.

In Singapore, all plant and equipment (except motor vehicles) qualifies for accelerated depreciation at 33.3% per annum. A company has the option to choose the straight line depreciation method with an initial allowance of 20% and an annual allowance ranging from six years to 16 years. Automated equipment and computers may be fully written off in the year of purchase.

In Malaysia, the normal rate of depreciation is 10% per year (for plant and machinery on a straight-line method) following an initial allowance of 20%. Industrial buildings are entitled to initial allowances of

10% in Malaysia (compared to 25% for Singapore) and annual allowances of 2% in Malaysia (compared to 3% in Singapore) on a straight-line basis.

Foreign Income

In both Singapore and Malaysia, foreign income is taxable only when remitted back to the respective country. Malaysia has signed a total of 31 "avoidance of double taxation agreements" with other countries. Malaysia's tax treaty policy aims at avoiding double taxation and encouraging foreign investment. Singapore has also signed numerous DTAs with other countries, the latest one being Vietnam. In addition to DTAs, both Malaysia and Singapore also grant unilateral relief in respect of income arising in Commonwealth countries, and for which both countries have no treaty arrangements for relief against double taxation.

Transfer Pricing and Anti-Avoidance Legislation

Transfer pricing refers to the price attached to dealings and transactions between related companies. By channelling their transactions through an associate company which is located in a tax haven, one can minimise tax incidence. Many countries have enacted anti-avoidance laws to tackle this issue. Examples are Section 33 of the *Tax Act* in Singapore and the 1986 Anti-Avoidance legislation in Hong Kong. In the case of Malaysia, there is close scrutiny in the transfer pricing area by the tax authorities.

Local Participation Requirements

The Singapore government freely permits 100% foreign ownership whereas the Malaysian government does not restrict the percentage of foreign ownership except where the corporation's activities involve dealings with the government. Where required, the level of local participation will generally be a minimum of 30% ownership by the indigenous Malay (Bumiputra). Additionally, up to 40% may be required to be held by other Malaysian citizens. The guideline of the New Economic Policy is 30% Bumiputra, 40% other Malaysians and 30% foreign. These guidelines have been relaxed with recent attempts to attract more foreign investment.

Personal Tax

The taxation framework of Penang State is governed by the Malaysia Federal Taxation framework. Table 5-1 highlights the differences between Malaysia and Singapore for basis year 1995.

TABLE 5-1
Comparative Tax Differences Between Malaysia and Singapore

	Malaysia	Singapore
Income Tax Rate:		
Minimum	2%	2.5%
Maximum	30%	30%
Capital Gain Tax	no *	no
Value Added Tax/Goods and Services	none	3%
Tax	yes	yes **
Stamp Duties	yes	yes
Import Duties		

* Except for real estate gains tax.
** Minimal, limited to items such as luxury goods, motor vehicle, alcohol and tobacco.

Income Tax

Income is taxed on a preceding year basis which means that income earned in the present calendar year is taxed in the following calendar year. For tax purposes, an individual is classified as either a "resident" or "non-resident". A person is considered to have a resident tax status when one has physically resided in Malaysia for at least 183 days in a calendar year; otherwise, one has a non-resident tax status. This is known as the physical presence test. Husband and wife are generally treated as separate taxpayers unless the wife elects for combined assessment.

Scope

Income tax is imposed on a territorial basis for individuals. All income derived in Malaysia, and foreign income received in Malaysia, are subject to Malaysian tax.

Business income, dividends, interest, rents, royalties, pensions and annuities are all taxable. In addition, any income which does not fall into the above categories will be subject to tax under the "catch-all" clause. However, non-resident employees (other than directors and public entertainers) are exempted for their Malaysian earned income if they are present in Malaysia for less than 60 days.

In addition, under the provision of tax treaties, the Malaysian tax authority might not tax employment income of a non-resident individual if the period of employment does not exceed 183 days and his/her remuneration is not borne by a permanent establishment in the country.

Personal Relief

Relief for personal, wife, medical expenses of parents, children and employee's EPF are available for deduction in arriving at taxable income.

Tax Rate

Resident individuals are taxed at progressive rates ranging from 2 to 30% on taxable income for basis year 1995. Non-resident individuals are taxed at a flat rate of 30% without any deduction for personal relief. In general, the "resident" status is preferred since it enables the expatriate to claim personal relief and permits taxation at progressive rates rather than a flat rate.

Capital Gains

Capital gains are not taxable except for transactions involving real estate or shares in a real estate company. Transactions involving real estate may result in taxable gains if the sale of property occurs within five years from the date of acquisition. Capital gains tax is imposed on a regressive basis from 30 to 5% which means that the longer the holding period, the lower the tax rate.

When a capital gains tax is levied, one is entitled to an exemption of RM5,000 or 10% of the gain, whichever is greater. A further one-time full exemption is given to gains from the sale of a personal residence.

Other Taxes

(i) ***Value Added Tax (VAT):*** There is no VAT currently administered in Malaysia. However, this form of indirect taxation is expected to be introduced when Malaysia progresses towards a developed country status.

(ii) ***Custom Duties:*** When individuals bring consumer items into the country, they may be liable for import duties on the goods depending on their weight or value.
(iii) ***Sales and Service Tax (SST):*** Sales tax is charged on some imported goods and certain manufactured goods ranging from 5 to 10%.

Miscellaneous

There are other taxes of a special nature which include the following:

(a) Stamp Duty;
(b) Service and Entertainment Tax;
(c) Road Tax; and
(d) Gaming Tax.

Withholding Tax

The payee is liable for withholding tax on payments made to non-residents on the following items:

(a)	Interest	15%;
(b)	Royalties	10%; and
(c)	Contract Services	20%.

There is no withholding tax on interest when the interest is attributable to a business carried out in Malaysia by a non-resident individual. The definition of royalties does not extend to management fees unless the fees are for technical services.

Double Taxation Relief

Avoidance of double taxation is provided through bilateral tax treaties and unilateral relief. To date, Malaysia has concluded 31 tax treaties which includes Singapore. The aim is to avoid double taxation and encourage foreign investment. All Malaysian income remitted to foreign countries or foreign income remitted to Malaysia are covered in the treaties with the exception of the United States which is limited only to shipping and air transport income.

Income remitted from a non-treaty country can be avoided *via* unilateral relief which is granted by the Malaysian tax authority upon application. A resident can enjoy a credit on foreign tax paid which is limited to the lower of Malaysian tax on that income or 50% of the foreign tax suffered.

BUSINESS AND FINANCIAL INCENTIVES IN PENANG

The system of offering business incentives in Malaysia is controlled by the federal government. As such, the State Government of Penang is not at liberty to offer any additional business incentives to investors.

To assist investors, the federal government offers a wide range of tax incentives and facilities. The principal tax incentives are contained in the *Promotion of Investment Act*, 1986 and the *Income Tax Act*, 1967. Basically, the tax incentives can be classified under two categories: general incentives and special incentives.

General Incentives

The general incentives provided by the government include the pioneer status, investment tax allowance and reinvestment allowance. These incentives are offered mainly to attract investment in the manufacturing sector. However, they are also applicable across other industrial sectors in Penang.

(i) ***Pioneer Status:*** Pioneer status (PS) is the principal tax incentive for investment in Penang. Businesses that are likely to generate profit in the early years of their operations should consider taking advantage of this incentive.

A company granted PS will be exempted from paying corporate income tax on 70% of statutory income for five years. The tax relief period will commence from the production date as stated on the pioneer certificate issued by the Ministry of International Trade and Industry (MITI). The period of exemption can be extended to ten years if approved.

PS will only be granted to companies involved in manufacturing a "promoted product" or that undertake a "promoted activity" as determined by MITI. The list of promoted products and activities includes:

(a) Agricultural;
(b) Integrated agriculture;
(c) Processing of agriculture produce;
(d) Forestry and forestry produce;
(e) Manufacture of rubber products;
(f) Manufacture of palm oil, palm kernel oil products and their derivatives;
(g) Manufacture of wood;
(h) Manufacture of pulp, paper and paperboard;
(i) Manufacture of textile and textile products polyester staple fibres;
(j) Manufacture of clay-based, sand-based and other non-metallic mineral products;
(k) Manufacture of iron and steel and their products;
(l) Manufacture of non-ferrous metals and their products;
(m) Manufacture of machinery;
(n) Manufacture of transport equipment, components and accessories;
(o) Supporting products/services;
(p) Manufacture of electrical and electronic products, components and parts thereof;
(q) Manufacture of professional, medical, scientific, measuring equipment components and parts thereof;
(r) Manufacture of photographic, cinematographic, video and optical goods and components;
(s) Manufacture of plastic;
(t) Hotel business and tourist industry;
(u) Film industry; and
(v) Other miscellaneous activities.

The criteria for MITI to grant a PS to a company will be subjected to the nature of the projects. These projects should have a high value added, high local content, high technology and linkages. In order to qualify for PS, the promoted product or activity must satisfy at least two of these criteria.

(ii) ***Investment Tax Allowance:*** The investment tax allowance (ITA) is a similar incentive to the PS. However, ITA is an attractive incentive to capital-intensive projects or projects with long gestation periods.

A company granted ITA will be given an allowance of 60% in respect of qualifying capital expenditure incurred within five years from the date of approval of the incentive. The allowance can be used to offset 70% of the statutory income in the year of assessment. Any unutilised allowances can be carried forward to subsequent years until they are fully depleted. 30% of the statutory income will be taxed. The criteria used for granting ITA are similar to that of the PS.

(iii) ***Reinvestment Allowance:*** In line with the government's objective to encourage companies to reinvest their profits, a reinvestment allowance (RA) is offered. This incentive allows a RA of 50% of the capital expenditure incurred for approved activities.

The RA is given in addition to the normal capital allowances. Where a company has been granted RA, its adjusted income equal to the allowance will be exempted from tax. Dividends paid out of the tax-exempt income are also exempted from tax in the hands of the shareholders.

The RA is mutually exclusive from the PS and ITA insofar as the same product is concerned. A company can claim RA on expansion incurred after the expiry of its PS or ITA or on the expansion of its manufacturing of a product for which it does not enjoy PS/ITA even during the period that it has PS/ITA for some other product.

Special Incentives

In addition to the general incentives, special incentives are also provided by the government to promote certain specific objectives such as export, research and development, training, storage/treatment/ disposal of toxic and hazardous wastes, etc.

(i) ***Incentives for Export:*** Investors who intend to export their products, or undertake efforts to explore export opportunities for their products, can consider taking advantage of the following opportunities:

(a) ***Export Credit Refinancing (ECR) Scheme:*** The ECR scheme provides short-term credit at preferential rates of interest (currently at 6.5% per annum) to enable exporters to compete more effectively in the international markets. This scheme is operated by the commercial bank and the Central Bank will refinance those banks which have extended export credit to eligible exporters. Two types of facilities include the pre-shipment ECR (maximum period of financing is four months) and the post-shipment ECR (maximum period of financing is six months).

To be eligible for the ECR facility, the goods to be exported must satisfy the following conditions:

(1) They should not be listed in the "negative list" of MITI (list available at MITI);
(2) They should have a minimum value-added of 20%; and
(3) They should have a minimum domestic resource content of 30%.

Companies that do not fulfill conditions (2) and (3) can still apply for the ECR through the Central Bank on a case-by-case basis.

(b) ***Double Deduction of Expenses for Promotion of Exports:*** In order to promote the export of products made in Malaysia, expenses incurred on certain approved activities will be eligible for double deduction. These activities include overseas advertisement, export market research, supply of free samples abroad, etc.

(c) ***Double Deduction of Export Credit Insurance Premiums:*** To encourage exporters to penetrate into non-traditional markets, double deduction is allowed for premium payments in respect of export credit insurance that is insured with a company approved by the Ministry of Finance.

(ii) ***Incentives for Research and Development:*** The government has actively encouraged investors to venture into research and development. Tax incentives given to R&D activities include double deduction of revenue expenditure incurred through related activities. In addition, an income tax exemption of five years is given to approved research institutes or companies which are established to undertake R&D in a particular industry. This incentive also applies to any new technology-based companies. To further encourage R&D activities, approved research companies can be given a 100% research allowance on capital expenditures incurred within a period of ten years. This allowance can be used to offset statutory income of up to 70% per year. In addition, companies conducting in-house

R&D will be granted a research allowance of 50% of the qualifying capital expenditure subjected to similar annual deduction conditions.

(iii) ***Incentives for Training:*** To encourage companies to invest in the training of their employees, the government has granted double deduction on training expenses incurred through approved training courses. In addition, the government has also facilitated training through setting up the Human Resource Department Fund (HRDF).

(a) ***Industrial Building Allowance (IBA):*** This incentive is granted to a company which has incurred expenditures on buildings used for approved industrial training. The incentive consists of an initial allowance of 10% and an annual allowance of 2%.

(iv) ***Incentive for the Storage, Treatment and Disposal of Toxic and Hazardous Waste:*** The Government also provides incentives for investors to set up proper facilities for the storage, treatment and disposal of toxic and hazardous wastes. The PS will be available to companies which are engaged principally in these activities.

Companies who set up facilities to store, treat and dispose of their toxic and hazardous by-products will also be granted a special capital allowance at an initial rate of 40% and an annual rate of 20% for a period of five years.

Both categories of companies are eligible for import duty and sales tax exemption for machinery and equipment, and also for raw material and components.

Operational Headquarters (OHQ)

Similar to the OHQ incentives that exist in Singapore, the Malaysian Government also grants a 10% concessionary tax on statutory income. Qualifying services include general management and administration, business planning, technical support and training subsidiaries or related companies outside Malaysia. This incentive will be granted only to companies having a minimum paid-up capital of RM500,000 and who are committed to spend at least RM1.5 million a year.

Other Incentives

Besides the tax incentives provided by the government, Penang also offers the following:

(i) ***100% Ownership Structure*** (Please refer to Chapter 4 for details.)

(ii) ***Free Industrial Zones (FIZ) and Industrial Parks (IP):*** Investors needs are catered for by FIZs and IPs. FIZs are special zones reserved for export-oriented businesses while IPs are ideal for all types of industries including local, ancillary and support industries. In this respect, the Penang State Government is actively developing the Bayan Lepas IP and Bukit Minyak IP with land prices of RM11.50 psf and RM10 psf, respectively.

(iii) ***Good Support Infrastructure:*** Penang also offers good support infrastructure to investors. This includes the Penang Development Corporation (PDC) which combines the functions of Singapore's Trade Development Board, Economic Development Board, National Productivity Board, Urban Redevelopment Authority, Housing and Development Board, and Singapore Tourist Promotion Board. In addition, Penang also offers an international airport and seaport, and it has a good network of roads. In terms of education, culture, food and other entertainment, Penang is similar to Singapore and, thus, should make it more pleasant for Singapore investors to venture into the state.

COMPLIANCE REPORTING

Corporate Registration

An application for a proposed name of the intended company has to be made with the Registrar of Companies (ROC). Thereafter, on receipt of approval of the proposed name, the company must lodge its Memorandum of Association, the Articles of Association and certain documents with the ROC. After the payment of a registration fee, which depends on the amount of the company's authorised capital, a Certificate of Incorporation will be issued by the Registrar. This certificate is conclusive evidence of the existence of the company. The incorporation of a company takes two to four weeks.

The company must have a secretary and a minimum of two directors who must have their principal, or only place of residence, in Malaysia. Directors need not be shareholders of the company.

The company registration formalities in Penang appear to be similar to Singapore as provided in the *Singapore Companies Act*.

Filing Requirements

A duly audited profit and loss account must be presented at the company's Annual General Meeting (AGM) not later than 18 months from the date of incorporation. Subsequent to this, it must be presented at least once in every calendar year at intervals of not more than 15 months. An AGM must be held once in every calendar year. An annual return must be filed with the Registrar of Companies together with the audited accounts and the directors' report within one month of the AGM. A foreign corporation must file its annual accounts in addition to the annual audited accounts of its Malaysian branch.

Record Keeping Requirements

The *Companies Act* imposes an obligation on the directors to keep accounting and other records that will sufficiently explain the transactions and financial position of the company and enable the accounts to be audited. Transactions must be recorded within 60 days from completion. The accounting records and a register of directors, managers and secretaries of the company must be kept at the company's registered office in Malaysia.

Accounting Standards

The Malaysian *Companies Act* of 1965 sets out the statutory disclosure requirements of companies. The Act is generally the same as those of other Commonwealth countries. The accounting standards are promulgated by the Malaysian Association of Certified Public Accountants and the Malaysian Institute of Accountants, and these standards are generally based on International Accounting Standards.

Audit Requirements

Each company must appoint an approved company auditor. An audit is required on the company each year. The statutory audited accounts must be supported by a directors' report and the auditor's report certifying that the financial statements give a true and fair view. These accounts have to be presented to the shareholders for approval at the AGM.

CONCLUSION

Malaysia is expected to move towards general lower taxation across corporate and personal fronts. As a policy objective, a shift in tax structure from an income tax to a consumption tax would be in order as Malaysia progresses steadily towards the status of a newly industrialised economy.

BANKING AND LABOUR MARKETS

Chapter 6

The Banking System and Financial Facilities in Penang

BY
HAN Kwee Juan
Dave GOH Cheok Cheng

INTRODUCTION

THIS REPORT EXAMINES the banking system in Penang. The main areas of focus are the general structure of the banking system, banking regulations, and the types of banking facilities available in Penang. A comparison of the banking system in Penang and Kuala Lumpur is also provided.

Penang is one of the thirteen states in Malaysia. The federal government in Kuala Lumpur basically sets the guidelines and policies on banking in Malaysian states. The federal government through the central bank, Bank Negara Malaysia (BNM) and the *Banking and Financial Institutions Acts* 1989, provides the regulations for banks operating in any part of Malaysia. As such, these rulings also apply to Penang.

STRUCTURE OF THE BANKING SYSTEM

The banking system in Penang, like any other state in Malaysia, is subject to the overall supervision by BNM. It controls and administers the activities of commercial banks and other financial institutions. BNM is also responsible for maintaining the monetary and financial stability of the country. It acts as a financial adviser to the government, issues the Malaysian currency and enforces exchange control regulations.

Commercial Banks, Merchant Banks and Finance Companies in Penang

Commercial banks concentrate their activities in the traditional areas of financing trade, working capital and investment funds, and other areas of retail banking such as the issuance of credit cards and the provision of mortgage/car loans.

Most of the lending activities are directed at manufacturing, trading activities, building and construction, and property development. A proportion of the financing activities goes to the priority sectors, namely the bumiputra community, small scale enterprises and private housing for individuals.

There are a total of 14 commercial banks in Penang operating 116 branches. As shown in Figure 6-1, the number of local banks outnumbers foreign banks. There are a total of two merchant banks in Penang. All commercial banks in Penang provide services to two main categories of customers which include corporations and individuals.

FIGURE 6-1
Composition of Banks in Penang

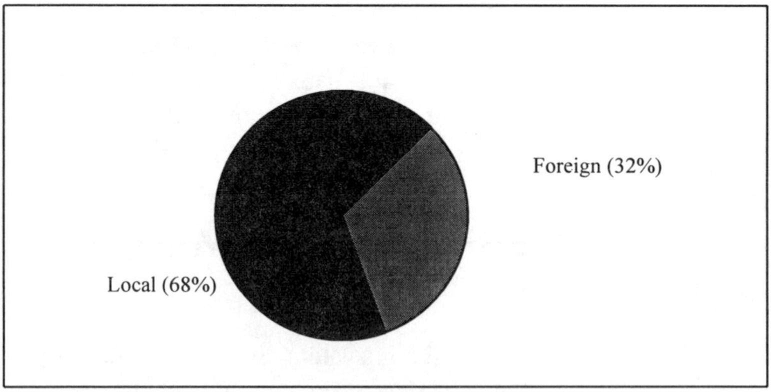

Most of the foreign banks in Penang set up their offices to support expatriate companies from their respective countries which operate in Penang. As such, these foreign banks provide a full range of commercial banking services such as trade services, remittance and receipt of foreign currencies, current account services, loans and deposits.

All the major banks have set up their main Penang branch near the Komtar area. Full banking facilities are available in these branches. Foreign banks are restricted to only a single branch in Penang while the local banks are allowed to set up branches in any part of Penang.

Islamic Banks

The Islamic banks are established based on Islamic principles to fill the void in the existing banking system, and to meet the banking and credit needs of the Muslim population according to the rules of the Syriah which prohibits interest. The Syriah, instead, provides such non-interest based concepts as Mudharabah, Murabahah, and many others which form the basis for the operations of Islamic Banks.

The Islamic banks in Penang carry out commercial banking activity based on the Islamic principles of banking and credit conforming with the Syriah, namely;

(i) ***Mudharabah:*** This is an agreement between a lender and an entrepreneur whereby the lender agrees to finance the entrepreneur's project on a profit-sharing basis according to a pre-determined ratio agreed upon in the negotiation. In the event of a loss, the lender bears the loss.

(ii) ***Musyarakah:*** This is a partnership for a specific business activity with the aim of making profits, whereby the lender not only provides the capital but may also participate in the management. As in the case of Mudharabah, all parties agree through negotiation on the ratio of distribution of profits generated from the business activity which need not coincide with the ratio of participation in the financing of the activity. However, in the event of a loss, all parties bear the loss in proportion to their shares in the financing.

(iii) ***Murabahah:*** This is the sale of goods at a price which covers the purchase price plus the profit margin agreed upon by both parties concerned. It transforms traditional lending activity into a sale and purchase agreement under which the lender buys the goods wanted by the borrower for resale to the borrower at a higher price agreed upon by both parties.

(iv) ***Al-Bai Bithaman Ajil:*** This is a variant of Murabahah whereby the borrower is allowed to defer settlement of the payment for the goods purchased within the period, and in the manner determined and agreed upon by both parties.

(v) ***Al-Ijarah:*** This is Syriah's concept of lease financing. Here, the bank purchases the asset required by the customer and then leases it to the customer for a given period. The lease rental and other terms and conditions are agreed to by both parties.

(vi) ***Al-Takjiri:*** This is a variant of the concept of Al-Ijarah which provides for the acquisition of the leased asset by the lessee.

(vii) ***Qard Hasan:*** This is defined as a "benevolent loan" which obliges a borrower to repay a lender the principal sum borrowed on maturity of the loan. However, it is left to the discretion of the borrower to reward the lender for his loan by paying any sum over and above the amount of the loan.

(viii) ***Al-Wakalah:*** This is an agreement between a customer and a bank in which the former appoints the latter as agent in undertaking a particular transaction.

(ix) ***Al-Kafalah:*** This is an agreement between a customer and a bank whereby the latter guarantees the fulfilment of the obligation of the former to a third party.

(x) ***Wadiah:*** This is an agreement to deposit an asset, excluding immovable fixed assets, in the custody of another party who is not the owner, or any such asset deposited with a non-owner for custody.

Merchant Banks

Merchant banks are designated to provide corporate finance and they offer a wide range of services including underwriting, investment advice, advice on mergers and acquisitions, corporate finance and the management of investment portfolios.

Finance Companies

Finance companies are allowed to attract deposits from the public but they are not allowed to offer current account facilities. The finance companies' main business includes financing of housing, hire purchase transactions, commercial, industrial and residential construction.

BANKING GUIDELINES AND REGULATIONS

Ministry of Finance and the Role of BNM

The Ministry of Finance and BNM are vested with powers to supervise the financial system in Malaysia under the *Banking and Financial Institutions Act*, 1989 which came into effect from October 1989. The *Act* regulates the conduct of banking and other specified categories of deposit-taking business and, in particular, covers the setting up of financial institutions, issues of licences and supervision of banking business.

BNM has the power to examine any books or documents of each licensed institution. The *Act* also allows the Minister to direct BNM to investigate the affairs of any institution suspected of carrying on business in a manner detrimental to the interest of the depositors or creditors, or a business which has insufficient assets. The main objectives of this supervision include the following:

(i) Protect the public interest, particularly the interest of the depositor;
(ii) Ensure that individual banks are safely and soundly managed so that the nation has a healthy and sound banking and financial system; and
(iii) Ensure that the financial institutions play a proper role in the economic development of the country.

BNM's philosophy is to promote monetary stability and a sound financial structure, and to influence the credit situation to the advantage of the country.

Banking licences are approved by the Minister of Finance upon recommendation of BNM. Applications must be submitted in writing to BNM and they will recommend to the Minister together with any conditions that need to be imposed on the licence.

The governing authorities of BNM have stated publicly that there are currently enough banks serving the country and, therefore, there is no need to issue any further commercial bank licences to foreign institutions. However, foreign banks are allowed to participate in the ownership of local banks up to 20% of the equity stake. As of December 1995, all foreign banks in Malaysia have been locally incorporated.

Capital Funds Requirement

Effective January 1990, the commercial banks, finance companies and merchant banks are required to comply with risk-weighted capital ratios of 7.25% by the end of 1990 and 8% by the end of 1992.

Locally incorporated banks must maintain a minimum paid-up capital and reserves of M$10 million while the foreign incorporated banks should not have less than M$25 million in their head office and they will have to follow the capital ratios.

Maintenance of Reserve Funds

Every licensed local institution is required to maintain a reserve fund before declaring any dividend from its net profits each year (after provision for taxation). Also, each institution can transfer to the reserve fund out of its net profit the following:

(i) an amount not less than 50% of the net profits so long as the reserve fund is less than 50% of the paid-up capital; and
(ii) an amount not less than 25% so long as the reserve fund is 50% of paid-up capital but less than 100%.

The amount to be transferred may be changed by BNM depending on the sufficiency of the funds for its operations in relation to the liabilities.

Repatriation of Profits

There is currently no restriction on the repatriation of profits for foreign banks so long as the audited accounts have been approved by BNM and the exchange requirements are met. However, since foreign banks will be locally incorporated, they will be subject to the maintenance of reserve funds requirements as set out above.

Additional Branches

In general, the banks (both local and foreign) need written consent from BNM for establishing or acquiring new branches in Malaysia, and outside Malaysia for local banks. The government feels that there are enough banks in Malaysia to serve the needs of individuals and corporations. Currently, it is extremely difficult for foreign banks to obtain approval for new branches.

Prohibited and Restricted Business

No licensed institution is allowed to engage in wholesale or retail trade, including import and export trade, except in connection with the realisation of security given. Also, no licensed merchant banks, finance companies or discount houses can accept money on deposit which is repayable by cheques/drafts or any other instruments drawn on the institution nor can they deal with foreign currency. The minimum and maximum amount, and period of deposit that can be received by a licensed institution, are controlled by BNM.

THE FINANCIAL MARKETS, FINANCIAL FACILITIES AND SERVICES

Financial markets in Malaysia are comprised of money markets, foreign exchange markets, capital markets and commodity markets. The money market essentially consists of primary and secondary markets for deposits, the inter-bank market and the treasury bill market. The foreign exchange market comprises inter-bank foreign exchange trading and the provision of foreign exchange services to corporate customers. The capital market deals with longer term financial assets, corporate stocks and shares, and public and private debts with maturities exceeding one year. Trading of corporate securities is done primarily in the Kuala Lumpur Stock Exchange (KLSE). The Kuala Lumpur Commodity Exchange (KLCE) was incorporated to transact in futures contracts in commodities and the Kuala Lumpur Tin Market (KLTM) is an open forum market for tin.

Since these markets are operating in the Malaysian capital, Kuala Lumpur, such activities are carried out on a limited scale in Penang. Banks will provide foreign exchange services to individuals but will refer companies which require such services to their head office in Kuala Lumpur.

Banks are free to set their deposit rates, and the rates are dependent on the free market. Banks are also free to set their lending rates. Lending rates are generally based on certain percentage points over the Base Lending Rate (BLR) of each bank. However, BNM's guidelines are that the minimum margin cannot be more than 4% above the BLR. All banks are free to quote their rates of exchange for all currencies.

Types of Financial Services Available

In terms of trade services, foreign banks have traditionally been strong in this area. Foreign banks typically assist in the payments of imports *via* issuance of letters of credit and receipt of funds of the exports through negotiation of letters of credit, for both multinational and local companies. In recent years, the local banks have gained substantial expertise in this area and are aggressively promoting their services to companies in Penang.

In Malaysia, BNM prohibits companies or individuals from opening any foreign currency accounts with banks. As such, banks in Penang do not offer any foreign currency current accounts or foreign currency deposits. The banks will provide remittance services for local and foreign currencies. Any companies or individuals in Penang who wish to remit any foreign currencies will need to execute a foreign exchange transaction (sell ringgit and buy the intended foreign currency) with a bank.

As for services in foreign exchange, loans and deposits, these are offered mainly in Kuala Lumpur. Banks in Penang will provide the "single window" contact and pass the transactions to their offices in Kuala Lumpur for processing and execution. In some cases, the companies are asked to contact the head office in Kuala Lumpur directly. There is no inter-bank foreign exchange trading or money market activities amongst banks in Penang.

Local currency loans and deposits are offered by all commercial banks in Penang. The loan rates are based on the Base Lending Rate (BLR) plus a certain percentage. The foreign bank branches in Penang are organised such that they have powers to temporarily increase the loan limit for their corporate customers based in Penang. This, however, does not apply to the locally incorporated banks. The local banks are centrally controlled by their main head office in Kuala Lumpur. As such, any requests for large increases in loan size will need to be referred to Kuala Lumpur for approval. The branches of the local banks in Penang are only vested with the powers to deal with loans up to a limit set by their main office. This credit limit varies from bank to bank.

All other commercial banks in Penang provide typical savings and current account services to individuals. The foreign banks are more aggressive in marketing loans such as personal and mortgage loans for individuals. In the area of credit card operations, individuals can apply directly to the branches of the foreign banks and local banks. The applications are processed by the branches in Penang and cards are issued in Penang.

The Islamic banks offer all the conventional banking services as well. Savings account holders are not entitled to a share of the bank's profit, but the bank at its discretion, may reward such savers with a token of their appreciation for the deposit of money with the bank.

CONCLUSION

In comparing Penang with Kuala Lumpur, Penang clearly has a distinct disadvantage. As explained earlier, all quotations for foreign exchange transactions are provided by the head office in Kuala Lumpur. Kuala Lumpur is the financial centre in Malaysia. There is an active money and foreign exchange market in Kuala Lumpur. Inter-bank foreign exchange and money market activities are carried out amongst branches of the various banks in Kuala Lumpur. Also, the proximity of factories in Kuala Lumpur to the local banks' head offices will allow finance managers of these factories to have constant interaction with the foreign exchange dealers to better understand the rate movements.

In addition, any new requests for loans from local banks need to be referred to Kuala Lumpur for approval. These constraints certainly cause a severe handicap for Penang as compared to Kuala Lumpur. Manufacturing firms which have set up factories in Kuala Lumpur will have easy access to the bank's head office. Therefore, the proximity to head office will allow companies to have easy access to bankers and the management of local banks which can make decisions on requests for loans. This will invariably shorten the time needed for approval of loans as compared to requests from Penang.

Since Penang is not intended to be a financial centre, and there is no good reason to duplicate Kuala Lumpur as a financial centre, banking development should be geared towards supporting the key growth sectors. Financial services should be concentrated on specialised funding requirements and speedy facilities for trade and investment. While effective telecommunications to the capital and regional financial centres are the urgent task for financial and banking reforms in Penang, we are less optimistic about Penang's role as a regional financial hub since Kuala Lumpur is currently working towards this goal.

Chapter 7

Labour Market Conditions and Wage Competitiveness

BY
Andrew KAN Mun Kit
Nelly NGADIMAN
POON Choon Gek
P. K. ABRAHAM
LEE Pau Sheng
NEO Kok Beng

INTRODUCTION

PENANG IS THE second smallest state in Malaysia with an area of approximately 1,031 sq. km. It is made up of two physical entities: one is Penang Island (293 sq. km.) and the other is Province Wellesley (738 sq. km.). The estimated population is 1,150,400. The projected average growth rate of the population is about 2% for the period 1990–96 and it will decrease gradually to about 1.9% in 1996–2000.[1]

Penang has changed dramatically from the agriculture and trade-based economy of the 1960s into an important industrial centre with a diversified and broad-based economic structure. While the rest of Malaysia is just turning to industrialisation, Penang is probably the first state to identify manufacturing as the key sector that would thrust the state into an ultra-modern developed state in the 21st century.

The manufacturing sector in the 1970s was generally narrow-based, and was dominated mainly by the electronic/electrical industry, the textile/apparel industry and the food/beverage industry. This pattern has continued into the

[1] *Penang into the 21st Century*, an official publication of the Penang State Government, October 1993.

1990s. Among these industries, the narrow production structure was most pronounced in the electronic/electrical industry where the manufacture of semiconductors dominated during the 1970s. During the 1980s, although other activities such as the manufacture of radio and TV sets, the production of electrical appliances and housewares, and cable and wire emerged as important sub-sectors, semiconductor production was still dominant. The manufacturing sector now accounts for nearly one-half of the state's gross domestic product as compared to only 13% in 1970.[2]

The dominance of the manufacturing sector in the state's economic activities has also made it the largest employer of the state's labour force. Operations in 16 out of 18 industries were labour-intensive during the 1970s. However, during the 1982 to 1988 period, at least one-half of the 16 industries which had begun as labour-intensive operations became more capital-intensive.[3] These trends suggest a rationalisation of production processes with respect to labour usage, and the move to more capital-intensive operations for higher productivity gains. In tandem with the economic performance, the rate of employment generation has surpassed the growth rate of the workforce. The unemployment rate was reduced to 4.9% in 1990.[4] Today, the manufacturing sector employs more than one-third of the total labour force and it is expected to continue to be the main employer for the state's workforce in the future.

LABOUR FORCE PARTICIPATION AND INDUSTRIAL EMPLOYMENT TURNOVER

Penang had a total population of 1 million in 1991 as compared to 900,000 a decade ago.[5] For the year 2000, it is projected that the population will increase to 1.4 million. Penang is blessed with a labour force that is predominantly young and well-educated with 65% of the

---

2 *Penang Investment Guide*, an official publication of Penang Development Corporation, June 1993.

3 *Penang Investment Guide*, an official publication of Penang Development Corporation, June 1993.

4 *Penang Investment Guide*, an official publication of Penang Development Corporation, June 1993.

5 *Investment in Penang, Malaysia*, an official publication of Penang Development Corporation, 1993.

population between the ages of 15 to 64. The median age is 30 for males and 29 for females. The labour force participation rate was estimated at 63.4% in 1990 with 86% participation for the male population and 44.5% for the female population (see Table 7-1). In 1991, Penang had a labour force of 469,000 of which 446,000 (95%) were employed in various industries. Approximately 46% of those employed were working in the manufacturing sector.

TABLE 7-1
Labour Force Statistics: 1990

Total Working Age Group (15–64) (thousands)	739.9
Labour Force (thousands)	469.0
Labour Force Participation Rate	63.4%
Male Labour Force Participation Rate	86.0%
Female Labour Force Participation Rate	44.5%
Total Employed (thousands)	446.0
Total Unemployed (thousands)	23.0 (4.9%)

Source: *Statistics, Penang Malaysia*, official publication by Penang Development Corporation, 1993.

As at April 1993, total employment in Penang was 483,928. Employment is expected to grow at the rate of 8.5% in 1993–94 with a slower growth of 5.1% in 1994–95. Skilled and unskilled workers together represent 73.2% of the total workforce.[6]

In terms of distribution, the Prai and Bayan Lepas Industrial Estates take up the main bulk of the workforce with each one employing over 42%. Employment at the new industrial sites on the mainland is growing at the rate of 15.3% which is almost twice the average growth of the entire region.[7] This has implications for factors such as infrastructure development, transport facilities and housing facilities as the growth centre shifts towards mainland Penang.

A distinct feature of industrial employment in Penang is the emphasis on two industry groups: the electronic/electrical and textile/garment industry groups. Both groups have a great influence on the growth of the workforce, turnover of employment and wages. However, employment in the metal products industry is increasing as factory

6 "Penang Annual Labour Market Report – Manufacturing Industry for the Year 1992–1995" by Federation of Malaysian Manufacturers, May 1993.

7 "Penang Annual Labour Market Report – Manufacturing Industry for the Year 1992–1995" by Federation of Malaysian Manufacturers, May 1993.

automation intensifies in response to the tight labour supply. The overall labour turnover rate for the year 1992–93 was 48.2% with the plastic products, paper products/printing works, and machinery/motor and bicycle parts showing over a 60% turnover rate (see Table 7-2). The Prai Industrial estate had the highest overall turnover rate at 54.6%. However, this could be due to the higher response from the high turnover rate industry groups such as the electronic/electrical industry. The turnover rate in Bayan Lepas is influenced greatly by the turnover rate of the electronic/electrical industry groups which accounted for 73.9% of the total employment in Bayan Lepas.

TABLE 7-2
Total Employment of Manufacturing Companies

Industry	Industrial Structure	01/01/93	01/01/94	01/01/95
Electronic/Electrical	42.8%	78,721	85,426	89,855
Textile/Garment	18.1%	33,291	36,126	37,999
Food Processing/Canning	4.3%	7,909	8,583	9,027
Processing of Agricultural Products	0.7%	1,287	1,397	1,470
Rubber-based Industry	4.8%	8,829	9,580	10,077
Timber-based/Wood Industry	2.0%	3,679	3,992	4,199
Metal Products	5.3%	9,748	10,578	11,127
Plastic Products	3.7%	6,805	7,385	7,768
Chemical/Fertiliser	1.8%	3,311	3,593	3,779
Paper Products/Printing Works	3.9%	7,173	7,784	8,188
Machinery/Motor & Bicycle Parts	4.5%	8,277	8,982	9,447
Feed-meals Industry	0.4%	736	798	840
Industrial Gases	0.0%	0	0	0
Others	7.7%	14,162	15,369	16,165
Total	100.0%	183,928	199,593	209,941
Growth Rate			8.52%	5.18%

Source: Federation of Malaysian Manufacturers, Secretariat to Manpower Monitoring Committee, HRDC, April 1993.

In terms of job category, the unskilled workers have the highest turnover rate at 75.1% (see Table 7-3). However, the turnover rate of unskilled male employees is higher than those of the female employees (not shown). The high turnover rate appears to reflect the tight labour supply situation created by high demand.

TABLE 7-3
Labour Turnover (by Location and Job Category): 1992–1993

Location	Managerial & Research	Supervisor & Technical	Clerical & Sales	General Workers	Skilled Workers	Unskilled Workers	Total
Prai	12.2%	21.4%	28.1%	81.6%	48.2%	76.3%	44.6%
Bayan Lepas	14.4%	21.1%	19.2%	52.5%	35.4%	80.0%	37.1%
Mak Mandin	8.3%	9.2%	14.2%	24.8%	9.8%	52.7%	19.8%
Others - Main Island	13.5%	10.7%	27.7%	52.5%	49.8%	54.2%	34.7%
Others - Island	12.9%	30.3%	50.0%	43.6%	36.9%	14.9%	31.4%
Total	**12.3%**	**18.5%**	**27.8%**	**51.0%**	**36.0%**	**55.6%**	**33.5%**

Source: Federation of Malaysian Manufacturers, Secretariat to Manpower Monitoring Committee, HRDC, April 1993.

LABOUR DEMAND AND SUPPLY IN THE MANUFACTURING SECTOR

The total demand for labour by the existing industrial companies in Penang is expected to reach a total of 26,013 in 1993–1994 (see Table 7-4). This figure will increase to 33,722, with an additional 7,709 workers needed by new companies.[8]

TABLE 7-4
Labour Demand (by Job Category)

Labour Demand	Managerial & Research	Supervisor & Technical	Clerical & Sales	General Workers	Skilled Workers	Unskilled Workers	Total
1992	615	2,027	783	756	11,556	2,630	18,367
1993	729	2,283	1,241	794	9,710	909	15,666
1994	424	1,123	1,061	521	2,131	5,087	10,347
Subtotal	1,768	5,433	3,085	2,071	23,397	8,626	44,380
Plus: Employment Expected from PDC New Projects							7,708
Total							**52,088**

Source: Federation of Malaysian Manufacturers, Secretariat to Manpower Monitoring Committee, HRDC, April 1993.

8 "Penang Annual Labour Market Report – Manufacturing Industry for the Year 1992–1995" by Federation of Malaysian Manufacturers, May 1993.

The demand for workers is largely determined by the electronic/electrical and textile/garment industries which, together, require 33,277 employees or 63.9% of the total demand for the years 1992 to 1994. The electronic/electrical industry group is expected to drop 45% between 1993–94.[9]

The slower growth in employment by the existing manufacturing companies in Penang may be attributed to the following:

(i) Existing companies have grown into a reasonable size and have matured, thus requiring fewer workers;
(ii) More companies have invested in labour-saving automation machinery and equipment;
(iii) Existing companies expansion, or modernisation, have been achieved through investment in expensive but less labour-intensive machinery;
(iv) The expansion in manufacturing capacity of the existing factories has slowed down due to world market conditions and the tight labour supply; and
(v) Some companies may have relocated their operations to where cheap labour is available.

From statistics and estimates provided by the Penang Education Department and PDC, the estimated supply of labour from secondary schools in Penang is as follows: 13,000 for 1993; 9,000 for 1994; 9,000 for 1995; and 13,000 for 1996. Assuming that all this output does not migrate to other states but directly enters the Penang labour market, these figures represent only 83% of the total additional labour required for 1993 and 87% for 1994.[10] The mismatch between supply and demand is obvious. The drop in supply in 1994 requires serious attention and immediate solution if the critical turnover of employment is to be prevented from becoming more serious.

Other factors that have had an impact on labour supply include:

(i) The absorption of labour by other service industries has not been taken into account in the analysis of supply/demand;

---

[9] "Penang Annual Labour Market Report – Manufacturing Industry for the Year 1992–1995" by Federation of Malaysian Manufacturers, May 1993.

[10] "Penang Annual Labour Market Report – Manufacturing Industry for the Year 1992–1995" by Federation of Malaysian Manufacturers, May 1993.

(ii) There were no statistics on the number of people returning to Penang after their college or university education;
(iii) The influx of labour to Penang from other states;
(iv) The competition for labour by neighbouring states; and
(v) The impact on labour supply after the completion of the north-south highway in late 1994.

STRATEGIES TO REDUCE LABOUR TURNOVER

Relocate Labour-Intensive Industries

To economise on the available manpower, and to utilise it in the most productive manner including reduced turnover, Penang should move away from labour intensive industries to skill intensive, higher value-added activities. This would ease the pressure on labour resources and ensure that resources are engaged in high productivity activities. In this case, the state should lobby for federal incentives to achieve this goal. Moreover, the state should also seek an active role in designing incentives so that they are in line with its goals.

Private Sector Participation in Human Resources Development Fund (HRDF)

The private sector should play a greater role in the retraining of the existing labour force through the HRDF. There also should be a national policy for retraining to enable at least 50% of the existing labour force to undergo retraining.

Apart from getting involved in vocational and tertiary training, the private sector should be encouraged to conduct in-house training, to provide practical training to new graduates, and to sponsor employees to further their studies in relevant disciplines.

Rising Wages and Profit-Sharing

The rigidities in the labour market should be removed through higher wages. This will increase labour mobility from labour surplus areas to Penang, attract more people such as skilled workers into the manufacturing sector, and attract those presently working in other countries to return. Besides higher wages, profit sharing is another important way to retain workers.

A Comprehensive Skills Development Programme

A comprehensive skills development programme should include the following:

(i) Flexibility in ensuring that new skills areas that were not identified are speedily incorporated into technical training programmes;
(ii) The retraining of workers which is necessary in a world of fast changing technologies;
(iii) The training of supervisory personnel in sound analytical, interpersonal and problem-solving skills, leadership abilities and technical skills;
(iv) The production of scientists, technologists and engineers for production processes as well as product design, development and R&D; and
(v) Stressing proficiency in English and mathematics within the general education system.

MANUFACTURING WAGE COSTS: PENANG VERSUS SINGAPORE

Because the manufacturing sector is a major contributor to Penang in terms of GDP (46%) as well as employment (46%) in the 1990s, it is important to focus on the wage costs[11] of the manufacturing sector. Singapore has a large manufacturing sector. In recent years, due to a rising cost of living which leads to higher business cost and wages, numerous companies have relocated their manufacturing operations to regional locations such as Batam, Johor, Penang and even as far away as China. However, Penang stands out as one of the most favoured locations due to its stable and efficient government, good industrial infrastructure and highly skilled workforce. Thus, Penang is a good alternative to Singapore as a manufacturing base for multinational companies.

A comparison of the wage costs between Singapore and Penang in the manufacturing sector is possible using published data for both Singapore[12] and Penang[13] for three years: 1992–1993 (actual), 93–94

[11] Wage costs are defined as employees' basic wages.

[12] *Digest of Singapore Labour Market Statistics 1991*, Singapore Institute of Labour

(projected), and 94–95 (projected). This data is discussed in more detail in the following sections.

Average Wage Costs in the 1990s

Wage rates for factory personnel vary depending on the type of industry, type of occupation, and skill level. According to the latest industrial survey, the median starting wage rate for skilled production workers ranges from RM12.50 (S$7.25)[14] to RM17.40 (S$10.09) per day while for unskilled production workers the range is from RM8.60 (S$4.98) to RM11.30 (S$6.55) per day.[15]

In 1992, the average salary for an engineer in Penang was RM2,253.00 (S$1,307.00); a technician was RM692.00 (S$401.00); a skilled production worker was RM467.00 (S$270.00); and an unskilled production worker was RM326.00 (S$189.00)[16] (see Tables 7-5 and 7-6).

In contrast, the average earnings of an engineer in Singapore (92–93) was RM5,199.00 (S$3,015.00); a technician RM2,052.00 (S$1,190.00); and a production worker RM1,983.00 (S$1,150.00) (see Table 7-7).

It should be observed that a simple comparison will not yield meaningful results as there are differences in cost of living, labour skills, and scope and efficiency of industrial infrastructure. As pointed out by the Chief Minister of Penang, Dr. Koh Tsu Koon, Singapore and Penang complement each other in industrialisation.[17]

Studies.

13 *Statistics, Penang Malaysia*, (p. 7 for the absolute figures) official publication by Penang Development Corporation, 1993. Percentages were provided by M. Singh, PDC.

14 At an exchange rate of S$0.58 to RM1.00.

15 *Investment in Penang, Malaysia*, official publication by Penang Development Corporation, 1993.

16 The average monthly wage costs may seem low in S$ units. However, it should be borne in mind that, in addition to wages and salaries, most companies also provide their employees with various benefits which generally include free medical treatment for staff members and their immediate family members, annual leave, provident fund contributions, bonuses and other allowances as incentives. All of these are not included in the basic wages reported here.

17 Dr. Koh Tsu Koon, Keynote Address to the NTU MBA Business Mission to Penang, February 1994.

TABLE 7-5
Penang's Basic Wages of Employees by Selected Industries and Occupation: 1992

Category of Employment	Electronic and Electrical (RM)	Textile and Garment (RM)	Fabricated Metal (RM)	Chemical (RM)	Plastic Product (RM)	Rubber Based (RM)	Paper Product (RM)	Average Salary (RM)
Engineer	2,150.00	2,750.00	2,100.00	2,300.00	1,970.00	2,250	2,250.00	2,253.00
Technician	690.00	650.00	720.00	770.00	695.00	550	765.00	692.00
Production Operators:								
Skilled*	15.00	13.50	18.50	18.00	14.00		16.00	467.00
Unskilled*	12.00	10.00	12.00	12.00	10.00	14.00	10.00	326.00
						10.00		

* Rates per day

Source: *Statistics, Penang Malaysia*, official publication by Penang Development Corporation, 1993.

TABLE 7-6
Penang's Average Monthly Nominal Wages by Occupation: 1992–1993 to 1994–1995

Average Wages Increase		Engineers	Technicians	Production Workers
In RM:	92–93	2,253	692	397
	93–94	2,436	756	428
	94–95	2,655	829	465
In S$:	92–93	1,307	401	230
	93–94	1,413	439	248
	94–95	1,540	481	270
In Percentage:	92–93	0	-	-
	93–94	8.1	9.3	7.8
	94–95	9.0	9.7	8.6

Source: *Statistics, Penang Malaysia*, official publication by Penang Development Corporation, 1993.

Figure 7-1 shows the trends of salary and wage growth in Penang for the various categories of employment.[18] Engineers and technicians can expect a salary growth rate of about 9%. However, the rate of wage increase has been slowing down over the years. This is due mainly to the relatively high basic salary that they command.

Skilled workers are expected to continue to experience an increase in wages which will rise from 2% in 1992 to 10.1% in 1994. This is due mainly to the emphasis on the capital intensive industries. Automation and the shift to high value-added industries require a large number of

[18] M. Singh, PDC, 1994.

skilled workers. Presently, skilled labour is in short supply and, consequently, such workers will benefit from substantial increases in salaries. However, unskilled workers will start to experience slower growth in salaries due to the shift away from labour-intensive industries.

TABLE 7-7
Singapore's Average Nominal Wages by Occupation: 1992–1993 to 1994–1995

Average Wages Increase		Engineers	Technicians	Production Workers
In S$:	92–93	3,015	1,190	1,158
	93–94	3,154	1,257	1,224
	94–95	3,299	1,327	1,302
In RM:	92–93	5,199	2,052	1,997
	93–94	5,438	2,167	2,110
	94–95	5,688	2,288	2,245
In Percentage:	92–93	4.6	5.6	6.4
	93–94	4.6	5.6	6.4
	94–95	4.6	5.6	6.4

Note: The following occupations are used as proxies for the Penang's categories:
(a) Professional, Technical, Administrative, Managerial, Executive and related workers (for engineers);
(b) Clerical, sales, service and related workers (for Technician); and
(c) Production, transport, and other manual workers (for production workers).

Source: *Singapore Yearbook of Labour Statistics, 1990*. The absolute figures for 1990 are used. The average growth rate from 1981 to 1990 is used to project all three years.

FIGURE 7-1
Projected Salary Growth

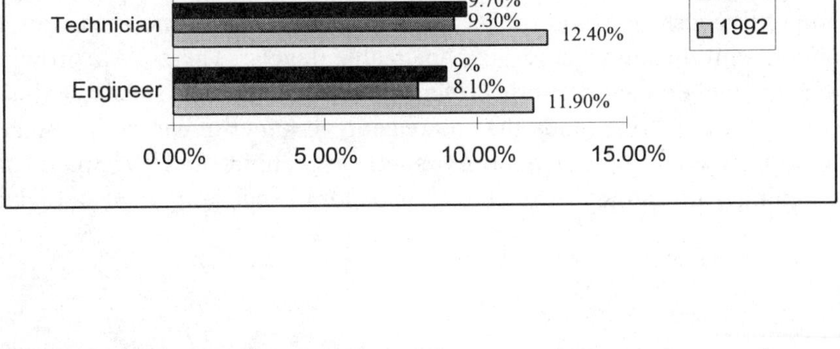

CONCLUSION

The key to sustained economic growth is to increase productivity. At present, PDC does not track productivity growth within Penang. Therefore, it is not possible to determine whether Penang's economic growth has been due entirely to increased inputs of capital, labour and materials, or to an increase in the efficiency of these inputs.

The increase in efficiency due to the manner in which capital, labour, materials and energy inputs are employed is commonly referred to as total factor productivity (TFP). TFP is computed as the difference between the rate of growth of output and the weighted average growth in capital, labour, material and energy inputs. Growth in TFP arises from the assimilation of new technologies, new techniques, and other measures that enhance the efficiency of production. The level of manufacturing TFP growth is important for Penang as it is a major source of growth in the long term.

Although higher output per worker can be achieved by continued capital investments, without the supporting increase in TFP or efficiency of input use, the increased capital employed per worker will tend to lower the rate of return on capital. This will eventually remove the incentive for new manufacturing investments in Penang. In the long run, sustainable real wage growth for workers in Penang will require a healthy rate of TFP growth. The improvement in TFP growth must be closely monitored to ensure that Penang's economic growth does not encounter labour cost pressures and a consequent decline in competitiveness.

Apart from the obvious need to monitor unit labour cost in Penang, there is also a need to monitor unit business cost. The unit business cost would measure the cost of doing business in Penang's manufacturing sector. It comprises unit labour cost, service charges (for distributive and telecommunication services etc.), and government indirect taxes and fees.

Penang's prospects for maintaining its current level of international competitiveness depends on its ability to take opportune measures to contain unit business cost at manageable levels. There is a growing concern that Penang's competitiveness is being eroded steadily by the shortage of labour and the increasing competitiveness of Asia's emerging economies. Countries such as China and Vietnam are becoming increasingly attractive to investors because of their abundant supply of relatively cheap labour, lower prices for land and office rentals, large domestic markets, and a host of fiscal and non-fiscal incentives that are being offered by their governments.

With the current full employment situation in Penang, labour is a scarce resource which can create limitations for expanding companies. This labour shortage can also operate to drive up wage costs. By keeping track of unit labour cost, the PDC will be able to monitor Penang's competitiveness and take timely corrective measures if real wages persistently outstrip productivity. In the long run, Penang's competitiveness will rest on its ability to make the transition from a production driven economy to an innovation driven economy, and on its ability to compete efficiently and successfully with the best in the world.

LABOUR LEGISLATION AND DEVELOPMENT

Chapter 8

A Comparative Analysis of Statutory Provisions and Collective Agreements

BY
LEE Kim Hua
TAN Tee Tee
Amy TSAI Yae-Ming

INTRODUCTION

IT WOULD BE incorrect to study the collective agreements (CAs) in Penang without first looking at the labour legislations covering the state. Unlike Singapore, Penang operates as a state under the federal government. The labour legislations governing Penang are thus those which govern Malaysia, except Sabah and Sarawak. Labour legislation has been enacted to cover the three main areas of labour standards, labour relations and employment.

LABOUR LEGISLATION AND TRADE UNIONS

Labour Standards

Labour standards ensure appropriate conditions for work and employment through the implementation of laws and regulations. They include minimum wage-fixing, labour inspection, occupational health and safety, and social security. The main legislation in this area includes the *Employment Act*, 1955; the *Wages*

Council Act, 1947; the *Employees Social Security Act,* 1969; the *Employees Provident Fund,* 1951; and the *Factories and Machinery Act*, 1967.[1]

Labour Relations

Labour administration promotes sound labour relations and supports collective bargaining. The laws provide guidelines for settling trade disputes and conflict resolution. The principal legislations are the *Trade Unions Act*, 1959, and the *Industrial Relations Act*, 1967.

Employment

The Ministry of Labour is involved in activities to promote full and productive employment through providing training and employment services. They also attend to the special problems of women and migrant workers. The chief legislations in this area are: the *Employment (Restriction) Act*, 1968; the *Employment Information Act*, 1953; and the *Private Employment Agencies Act*, 1981.

Some of the major labour enactments currently in force in Malaysia include the following:

(a) *Employment Act*, 1955
(b) *Wages Council Act*, 1947, and *Wages Regulation Orders*
(c) *Workmen's Compensation Act*, 1952
(d) *Workers (Minimum Standards of Housing) Act*, 1966
(e) Labour Code (F.M.S. Cap 154) and equivalent Labour Codes for the respective states
(f) *Children and Young Persons (Employment) Act,* 1966
(g) *Weekly Holidays Act*, 1950
(h) Internal Security (Registration of Labour) Regulations, 1960
(i) *Employment Information Act*, 1953
(j) South Indian Labour Fund Ordinance, 1958
(k) *Industrial Relations Act*, 1967
(l) *Trade Unions Act*, 1959

---

1 Aminuddin, Marilyn, *Malaysian Industrial Relations*. Singapore: McGraw Hill, 1990; Ayadurai, Dunston, *Industrial Relations in Malaysia: Law and Practice*. Singapore: Butterworths Asia, 1992; Mills, Charles Patrick, "Industrial Disputes Law in Malaysia". *Malayan Law Journal*, 1984; and Wu, Min Aun, *The Industrial Relations Law of Malaysia*. Singapore Heinemann Educational, 1982.

(m) *Factories and Machinery Act,* 1967
(n) *Employees Social Security Act*, 1969
(o) *Pensions Act*, 1980
(p) *Private Employment Agencies Act*, 1981
(q) *Employees Provident Fund Act*, 1951
(r) *Public Service Tribunal Act*, 1977

From the various acts listed above, the *Trade Unions Act*, 1959, the *Employment Act*, 1955 and the *Industrial Relation Act*, 1967 constitute the main body of laws governing industrial relations in Penang.

The *Employment Act* lays down provisions to protect workers from exploitation, and to ensure minimum benefits for all workers covered by the Act. It governs those who earn less than RM1,250 per month. The benefits provided include termination and maternity benefits, the right to a weekly rest day, annual leave and sick leave.

The *Trade Unions Act* seeks to control the activities of trade unions so that they can develop in an orderly and peaceful manner. This is done by laying down the rules and regulations which unions are required to follow.

The *Industrial Relations Act* regulates the relations between employers and workmen and their unions and lays down rules to help prevent disputes between the two parties, thus ensuring peaceful industrial relations as much as possible.

Trade Unions in Penang

The number of trade unions in Malaysia as of September 1991 is shown in Table 8-1.

The number of unionised workers constitutes only about 10% of those eligible to be union members. This, however, does not diminish the importance of the unions as the standards set in the unionised environment generally influence employment conditions in similar enterprises within the same locality.

It is interesting to note that workers in the electronics industry in Penang are not unionised. This may be a result of the proactive attempts by companies to prevent their workers from joining trade unions. Aminuddin (1990) suggests that many companies take positive long-term steps to reduce or eliminate the need for their workers to join trade

TABLE 8-1
Profile of Trade Unions in Malaysia

Sector	No. of Unions	Membership
Private	241	362,892
Statutory Bodies	85	88,823
Government	135	204,920
	461	656,635
	18	644
Employers Unions	3	-
Federation of Trade Unions		
Total	**482**	**657, 279**

Source: Sivagnanam, S., Human Resources Management and Industrial Relations. Seminar on "Investment Opportunities in Penang", 1994.

unions.[2] These measures include the following:

(i) Provide higher wages and better benefits than those prevailing in comparable companies within the same locality;
(ii) Involve employees at all levels of decision-making and effectively implement an open-door policy by the elimination of barriers of status such as calling each other on a first-name basis;
(iii) Offer training and development, and a measure of security of tenure because investment in training by the company shows employees that their development is valued; and
(iv) Develop a climate of trust and loyalty in the organisation. Through regular feedback techniques, management can gather information about factors that cause dissatisfaction. Workers' problems, however trivial, would be attended to and, as much as is possible, solved with the help of the organisation's management. If resolution is not possible, workers would be told the reason. There is emphasis on training supervisors to be effective, especially in terms of ensuring they are fair in their duties, evaluating performance, and giving praise and punishment.

---

2 Aminuddin, Marilyn, *Malaysian Industrial Relations*. Singapore: McGraw Hill, 1990.

THE INDUSTRIAL RELATIONS SYSTEM AND THE COLLECTIVE BARGAINING PROCESS

Nearly all industrial relations systems are tripartite. This means that they include the employer, employees and the government. In Malaysia, the Ministry of Labour represents the government in the industrial relations system.[3] The Congress of Unions of Employees in the Public and Civil Services (CUEPACS) and the Malayan Trade Union Congress (MTUC) are the major employee representatives while the Malaysian Employers Federation makes up the third party. Discussion on the success and failure of the labour movement in Malaysia is beyond the scope of this paper but several insightful sources are available in the literature.[4]

The collective bargaining process in Malaysia is similar to that of Singapore. Collective bargaining can take place between a single employer and a union, or between a group of employers and a union. Multi-employer bargaining is found where an employer's association or union exists. The procedure for collective bargaining is laid out in the *Industrial Relation Act* (s. 13). Much of what must be contained in the collective agreement is similar to that of Singapore. A major difference is that the duration of agreement in Malaysia must be for at least three years while in Singapore it is between two to three years.

COMPARISON OF STATUTORY PROVISIONS AND COLLECTIVE AGREEMENTS BETWEEN SINGAPORE AND PENANG

General Comparison

A comparison of the statutory benefits/provisions to be included in collective agreements according to the labour legislations of Singapore and Penang can be found in Appendix 8-1. A comparison of the collective agreements of the manufacturing sector for Singapore and Penang are also included in Appendix 8-1. While the Singapore National

---

3 Khan, Md. Muinuddin, *Labour Administration: Profile on Malaysia*. Bangkok: International Labour Organisation, 1989.

4 See for example, *Labour-Management Cooperation: A Key to Productivity Promotion*. Tokyo: Asian Productivity Organisation, 1992; and Mills, Charles Patrick, "Industrial Disputes Law in Malaysia". *Malayan Law Journal*, 1984.

Employers Federation conducts yearly surveys and publishes summaries of the collective agreements in Singapore,[5] it is difficult to find information of a similar format in Penang. Collective agreements are also confidential documents which companies are generally unwilling to disclose. However, four copies of expired collective agreements were collected through the assistance of the Penang Development Corporation. Only two are recent enough to be of use. Comparisons of the provisions in the collective agreements are thus based on a small sample of two collective agreements from Penang while the information on Singapore collective agreements are those summarised in the latest SNEF publication for 1993.

A total of 44 fringe benefits provided in the collective agreements of Singapore and Penang, both statutory and non-statutory, were compared. There were no significant differences between the provisions of five fringe benefits while another seven could not be compared due to differences of interpretations. Of the remaining 32 benefits, Singapore CAs generally had more favourable provisions for employees for 19 of the benefits while Penang had better provisions for the other 13 benefits.

Specific Comparisons

A detailed comparison of the five benefits are discussed in this section. For ease of reference, the benefits are listed as they appear in the table. It should be noted that the comparison is based on data of different sizes.

(i) ***Flexible Wage Increment:*** Only Singapore companies provide for this benefit. This is expected as Malaysia is just moving into the flexible wage system. The industry-wide average in Singapore is 3.7%.

(ii) ***Annual Leave:*** Penang companies are more generous in annual leave granted to employees. The range of 12 to 22 days per year as compared to 10 to 17 days in Singapore is also in line with the more generous provisions in the Malaysian *Employment Act.*

(iii) ***Hospitalisation:*** A range of 60 to 90 days of hospitalisation leave may be granted to employees in Penang, with more days given on a case by case basis. This is more generous than Singapore companies which grant a maximum of 74 days (mode is 60 days). There is

---

5 *A Comparative Guide to Collective Agreements in the Manufacturing Sector 1992–93*. Singapore: The Singapore National Employers Federation, 1993.

no difference in the provisions in the *Employment Act* of both countries.

(iv) ***Shift Allowance:*** Singapore companies are more generous with this benefit. The lowest amount of $2.85 for a split shift allowance is higher than the maximum amount of RM3 that a night-shift worker receives in Penang, not taking the exchange rate and relative cost of living into consideration.

(v) ***Work on Rest Day/Public Holiday:*** Although both Singapore and Penang companies pay according to the *Employment Acts* for work on rest days and public holidays (i.e. twice the normal wage rates), Penang companies pay 4.5 times the hourly rates for overtime work on such days. This is more favourable than the three times the normal rate paid by Singapore companies.

(vi) ***Outstation Reimbursement/Allowance:*** Since most Singapore companies do not send their bargainable employees overseas, no such provisions are made. Penang companies have very generous allowances of up to RM55 per night with additional payment for meals.

(vii) ***Retirement Age:*** In line with the raising of retirement age through legislation, Singapore companies have been gradually changing the compulsory age to 60 years. Malaysia has not introduced legislation on retirement age but Penang companies, however, are still maintaining the retirement age at 55 years for men and 50 years for women. The higher retirement age in Singapore is more favourable to employees.

(viii) ***Retrenchment Benefit:*** Singapore companies are more generous in giving 1 month's pay for each year of completed service prior to retrenchment. Companies in Penang may pay as low as 20 to 23 days pay for each year of completed service.

(ix) ***Long Service Benefit:*** While companies in Singapore do not state specifically the benefits available to long-serving employees, one Penang company states that employees who have worked for 20 years continuously will be granted three months paid leave.

(x) ***Attendance Allowance*** **and** ***Productivity Incentive Allowance:*** Companies in Singapore provide incentives for attendance and productivity. This is in line with the government's objective of boosting the country's competitiveness rating among investors. Such incentives are not evident in the collective agreements of Penang. However, some companies (in particular, those which have "migrated" from Singapore) have started including such practices in their contracts of employment.

In summary, the benefits which are more favourable in Penang are annual leave, hospitalisation, work on rest days and public holidays, outstation reimbursement/allowance, and long service benefits. Benefits which are more favourable in Singapore are flexible wage increments, shift allowance, retirement age, retrenchment benefits, and attendance allowance and productivity incentive payments.

CONCLUSION

It is not possible to make general conclusions due to the limited data analysed. However, a few observations can be made about the collective agreements that exist in Singapore and Malaysia.

The Malaysian legislation and collective agreements have more specific provisions and thorough coverage. This does not necessarily translate into better or more favourable conditions for employees. In this instance, we do not refer to a comparison of the quantum of wages or benefits but rather to the number of benefits accorded them. The Malaysian employee is entitled to a specific amount when it comes to allowances which are covered in the agreements and this leaves no doubt as to how much he will receive. The figures in the CAs serve as a minimum but, as we found out in the course of meeting the employers, the actual benefits and allowances usually exceed the stipulated amount. This also serves to minimise the number of disputes that may arise.

Malaysia, and Penang in particular, faces the enviable problem of a labour shortage and almost full employment. Employees do not have to worry about retrenchment even though this is provided for. The result is the need for employers to provide better benefits if they wish to retain workers. One also notices that most employers discourage unionisation of workers by providing non-unionised workers with better wages and benefits than those that belong to unions. The wage spiral that is evident today in Penang is due in part to the unionised workers trying to be on par in terms of wages and benefits with the non-unionised workers.

If there is one conclusion that can be made, it is that the Malaysian industrial relations system and its present environment are stable and, thus, favourable for investors. One can safely assume that as workers become more educated and see the benefit of collaboration, instead of confrontation, the industrial relations environment will evolve for the better.

APPENDIX 8-1
Comparison of Labour Legislations and Collective Agreements in Singapore and Penang

Item	Provision in Singapore Legislations	Provision in Malaysia Legislations	Singapore Collective Agreements	Penang Collective Agreements	Favourable Singapore (S) or Favourable Penang(P)?
Flexible Wage Increment	No specific provision.	No specific provision.	Range of 2 to 5.5% service increment with an average of 3.7%.	Nil	S
Annual/ Service Increment	No specific provision.	No specific provision.	Annual increment range from 2.0 to 6.0% with an average of 4.2%.	Range from 3.8 to 8.4%.	P
Annual Wage Supplement (AWS)	Not more than one month's wages for fixed AWS. Variable payment subject to negotiation.	No specific provision.	Range from 1 to 2.8 months of basic salary with an average of 1.1 months. Mode of 1 month.	Nil	S
Compassionate Leave	No specific provision.	No specific provision.	1–5 days for death of family members with average of 3 days. 1–4 days for critical illness with average of 2 days.	2–3 days for death of immediate family member. 2 days for emergency leave.	S
Maternity Leave/Grant	8 weeks with condition of minimum 180 days worked before confinement. Only for first three children.	8 weeks with condition of minimum 90 days worked before confinement.	Most provision according to E. Act.	Same as Singapore except for limited to first 5 surviving children.	P
Marriage Leave	No specific provision.	No specific provision.	Range of 1–10 days for first marriage with an average of 4 days.	3 days for first marriage.	S

APPENDIX 8-1 (cont'd)

Item	Provision in Singapore Legislations	Provision in Malaysia Legislations	Singapore Collective Agreements	Penang Collective Agreements	Favourable Singapore (S) or Favourable Penang(P)?
Sick Leave	14 days paid sick leave per year.	Same	Range of 14–30 days per year with an average of 16 days. Mode 14 days.	Up to 2 yrs: 14 days. 2–5 yrs: 18 days. More than 5 yrs: 22 days. More than 10 yrs: 30 days.	P
Long Term Illness Leave	No specific provision.	No specific provision.	Most common leave pattern: 1st 6 mths: full pay. 2nd 6 mths: half pay. 3rd 6 mths: no pay.	Either same as Singapore or in 5-month intervals instead of 6.	No significant difference.
Union Day Leave	No specific provision.	No specific provision.	38.2% provided for union officials to attend Union's Anniversary Day celebrations.	Nil	S
Unpaid Overseas Leave	No specific provision.	No specific provision.	3 to 6 months may be granted after 3–5 years of service.	Provided at discretion of company.	S
Funeral Leave/Grant	No specific provision.	No specific provision.	$100 to $500 for death of immediate family.	RM500 to immediate family members for death of employee.	Cannot be compared.
Hospitalisation	Up to 60 days paid leave for hospitalisation.	Same	Range of 28 to 74 days with average of 59 days. Mode is 60 days.	From 60 to 90 days. More may be granted on a case by case basis.	P
Surgical and Specialist Benefits	No specific provision.	No specific provision.	Range of $1000 to $5000 with an average of $2518. Mode $2000.	Look under Medical.	S

APPENDIX 8-1 (cont'd)

Item	Provision in Singapore Legislations	Provision in Malaysia Legislations	Singapore Collective Agreements	Penang Collective Agreements	Favourable Singapore (S) or Favourable Penang(P)?
Dental Treatment	No specific provision.	No specific provision.	Range from $20 to $200 with average of $77.90. Mode $100.	Look under Medical.	S
Annual Bonus	No specific provision.	No specific provision.	Look under Annual Wage Supplement.	2 months basic salary.	P
Shift Allowance	No specific provision.	No specific provision.	$3.80 for 2nd shift. $7 for third shift. $2.85 for split shift.	RM2 for evening shift. RM3 for night shift.	S
Acting Allowance	No specific provision.	No specific provision.	$4.50 to $10 per day.	RM5 to RM10 per day or 1 increment of salary scale.	S
Meal Benefit	No specific provision.	No specific provision.	Free or subsidised meal, allowance, or reimbursement provided.	RM4 for lunch.	S
Educational Incentive/Study Leave/Benefit	No specific provision.	No specific provision.	Nil	Leave to take examinations at discretion of company.	No significant difference.
Work on Rest Day/Public Holiday	Not less than twice daily rate plus overtime pay calculated at this rate.	Same	According to E. Act.	Twice normal rates. Overtime paid at 4.5 times hourly rate on Public Holidays only.	P
Outstation Reimbursement /Allowance	No specific provision.	No specific provision.	Nil	Overnight at RM55 per night. Otherwise, RM2 for breakfast, RM4 for lunch and RM5 for dinner. RM3 for breakfast, RM4 for lunch and RM5 for dinner. RM28 for lodging.	P

APPENDIX 8-1 (cont'd)

Item	Provision in Singapore Legislations	Provision in Malaysia Legislations	Singapore Collective Agreements	Penang Collective Agreements	Favourable Singapore (S) or Favourable Penang(P)?
Retirement Age	60 years	No specific provision.	55 to 60 years with 60 years being most common (74.3%).	Male 55 years, Female 50 years. 55 years	S
Retirement Benefits/ Gratuity	Condition of minimum 5 years continuous service. No specific benefit provided.	No specific provision.	16% of CAs provided additional benefits in addition to CPF contributions.	Contribution to EPF at: 1st 5 years at statutory rate required by EPF Ordinance. 5 years and above, 15% of basic monthly salary. 15% of basic monthly salary throughout.	P
Retrenchment Benefit	Condition of minimum 3 years continuous service. No specific benefit provided.	No specific provision.	1 month for each year of completed service is common.	1 to 15 years – 20 days pay for each completed year of service. 15 years and above – 23 days pay for each completed year of service. 1 month's pay for each completed year of service.	S

APPENDIX 8-1 (cont'd)

Item	Provision in Singapore Legislations	Provision in Malaysia Legislations	Singapore Collective Agreements	Penang Collective Agreements	Favourable Singapore (S) or Favourable Penang(P)?
Termination benefit	Notice period to be agreed in CA. No notice needed for dismissal due to misconduct but inquiry must be conducted before dismissal.	Same	Nil.	2 weeks to 1 month notice. According to E. Act.	Cannot be compared.
Medically Boarded Out Benefit	No specific provision.	No specific provision.	$5,000 to $10,000 with minimum 2 to 5 years of service.	1 month's salary for each year of service.	Cannot be compared.
Death/ Incapacitation Benefit	Provided under Workmen's Compensation Act. Monthly earnings times multiplying factor (dependant on age). Minimum $26,000 and maximum $78,000.	Provided under Workmen's Compensation Act. Monthly earnings times 45 or RM14,400 whichever is less.	According to legislation.	Compensation according to legislation. For disability not due to negligence of employee, company will provide alternative employment.	P
Long Service Benefit	No specific provision.	No specific provision.	Some form of benefit is provided for employees with at least 3 years of service.	3 months paid leave for at least 20 years of continuous service.	P
Attendance Allowance	No specific provision.	No specific provision.	$25 to $50 per month.	Nil	S
Productivity Incentive Payment	No specific provision.	No specific provision.	3.8% of CAs provide for some form of incentive payment.	Nil	S

APPENDIX 8-1 (cont'd)

Item	Provision in Singapore Legislations	Provision in Malaysia Legislations	Singapore Collective Agreements	Penang Collective Agreements	Favourable Singapore (S) or Favourable Penang(P)?
Apparel	No specific provision.	No specific provision.	Average of 3 sets of uniform per year when necessary.	2 –3 sets of uniform when needed.	No significant difference.
Safety Cloth-ings/ Shoes	Extensive provisions under Factories Act.	Extensive provisions under Factories and Machinery Act.	As per legislation.	As per legislation.	No significant difference.
Insurance	No specific provision.	No specific provision.	Employees covered by group insurance. Sum insured per em-ployee averages $10,000 to $15,000.	Covered by group insurance. No information on sum in-sured.	Cannot be compared.
Advanced Festive Pay-ment/ Festive Loan	No specific provision.	No specific provision.	Half to a month's pay before re-spective festivals.	Half a month's pay before respective festivals.	No significant difference.
Co-operative Shares	No specific provision.	No specific provision.	$10 to $23 to purchase NTUC FairPrice Co-operative Shares.	Nil	S
Machine Allow-ance	No specific provision.	No specific provision.	$20 to $60 for use of certain ma-chine (e.g. microscope or driving heavy duty vehicles.)	Nil	S
Other Loans	No specific provision.	No specific provision.	3.2% of CAs provide for housing loan of RM8,000 repayable over 4 years at 5% interest.	Nil	S

Chapter 9

Human Resource Management

BY
LOI Kheng Seong
YEO Kian Sin
CHAN Siew Koon

INTRODUCTION

THIS PAPER AIMS to present the findings concerning skills development in Penang. It also seeks to compare and to contrast the strategies and programmes adopted by Singapore's Skills Development Fund (SDF) with those of Malaysia's Human Resource Development Fund (HRDF).

The study begins with an overview of manpower training and development in Penang. Penang's economy has grown dramatically over the past two decades and faces the problem of manpower shortages, and the mismatch between job requirements and labour skills. In order to solve these problems, the state government has adopted several skills development strategies.

The paper also gives an explanation of the need for the HRDF in Penang and the concept of market failure is briefly described. The paper then compares the strategies and activities of the SDF and HRDF. The paper concludes with an examination of the rationale for why the SDF and HRDF are necessary to prevent market failure.

OVERVIEW OF MANPOWER TRAINING AND DEVELOPMENT IN PENANG

Penang has experienced phenomenal growth during the 1980s and early 1990s because of rapid industrialisation and the transformation from a commodity to a manufacturing-based economic state. Economic growth has increased exponentially with the encouragement of the state government to attract foreign investments. As Penang attempts to become a highly sophisticated technology manufacturing economy, skilled manpower shortages, and the mismatch between job requirement and skills for the manufacturing and service sectors have been aggravated. Therefore, the development of skilled human resources is a key issue in meeting the needs of a high technology environment.

Realising the importance of training, the state government has taken actions to promote and encourage educational and training programmes to satisfy the quantitative demands imposed on its human resources by the industries. The emergence of private technical schools, training institutions and twinning programmes in Penang indicates a greater awareness of the benefits of higher education, and the need for formalised experience and skills. In addition to these institutions providing basic education and training to school leavers, an application-based training centre, Penang Skills Development Centre (PSDC), was set up to provide retraining or upgrading of the existing workforce. This paper focuses on skills upgrading of the existing workforce. Therefore, emphasis is placed only on the PSDC because it is the first, and the only, industry-led training institution in Malaysia.

The PSDC is a non-profit society which aims to facilitate effective utilisation of resources from amongst the manufacturing and service sectors. Presently, the PSDC provides four types of training namely, technical skills, management skills, manufacturing skills and continuing education. The breakdown of the types of training courses provided by PSDC in 1993 was 20% for management, 20% for technical, and the remaining 60% for manufacturing and continuing education courses. The PSDC has 55 corporate members at the moment, and has set up five laboratories and two workshops to provide hands-on training. The five laboratories cover computers, programmable automation literacy, industrial automation technology, electronic and microprocessing PCs. The two workshops relate to precision and basic machining training.

In addition, to provide training in the emerging skills, the PSDC has plans for two new laboratories pertaining to surface mount technology and vacuum technology.

Over and above these training facilities, the federal government has provided some incentives to encourage upgrading of skills, improvement of productivity and quality of the workforce. These notable incentives include the following:

(i) The double deduction of expenses incurred on approved training is given to the manufacturing and non-manufacturing sectors. Employers enjoy the double deduction for expenses incurred for training an employee provided that he/she is trained at one of the 12 approved and gazetted institutions. This scheme is only applicable to those companies which employ less than 50 Malaysian workers.

(ii) An industrial building allowance is granted to a company which has incurred expenditures on buildings used for approved industrial training with an initial allowance of 10% and an annual allowance of 2%.

(iii) For those companies with more than 50 Malaysian workers, some assistance is provided by the HRDF. These companies, however, have to contribute to the HRDF at the rate of 1% of the employees contribution. The employers can recover at least 40 to 70% of the total contribution to the HRDF.

Penang is putting much effort into upgrading its human resources in order to create a conducive climate to attract foreign investors through training schemes available in the PSDC and training incentives.

SKILLS DEVELOPMENT STRATEGIES IN PENANG

In order to utilise human resources more effectively, the state government has formulated seven human resource development strategies. Four of the strategies emphasise skills development and training of employees. The four strategies are:

(i) ***Developing a Comprehensive Technical Skills Development Programme:*** This programme will give attention to areas such as overall skills development; movement of labour to skill-intensive and high value-added industries; streamlining the roles of the private and public training system; postgraduate technical education and skill development at the national level.

(ii) ***Fostering Industry Cooperation in Training and Forging Links Between Industry and Training Institutions:*** A few steps have been taken by the state government to achieve this objective. The state government has pooled the resources of key industries to set up training facilities such as PSDC, and it has encouraged firms to utilise the HRDF.

(iii) ***Pursuing Further Improvements in Formal and Non-Formal Training Arrangements:*** The state government will work closely with the relevant federal ministries and agencies to improve formal and non-formal training arrangements for skills development.

(iv) ***Re-establishing Penang as a Centre for Learning and Training:*** Penang will re-establish its role as a regional centre and, therefore, provide better infrastructure and facilities.

RATIONALISING THE NEED FOR A HUMAN RESOURCE MANAGEMENT FUND

With the rapid development of the manufacturing sector in Penang, there is an increased demand for a skilled and trained workforce to meet the stringent requirements of industry. The shortage of skilled labour is serious and the high turnover of skilled employees strains the economy. Training of workers is costly and many companies resort to "pinching" trained employees from other companies as a cheap means of getting skilled labour. This acts as a disincentive to train workers. It results in market failure because firms would rather "pinch" workers than train them.

To prevent market failure, government intervention with plans such as the implementation of the HRDF scheme was necessary. Implementation of this scheme requires companies with more than 50 employees to contribute to the fund regardless of whether they participate in labour training. The scheme forces the big companies (more than 50 employees) to train their employees in order to enjoy the benefits of the scheme. Therefore, the movement of trained employees from one company to another has no cost impact on the trainer company because all the companies are required to contribute towards training cost. In addition, the scheme also helps in maintaining the morale of employees.

A COMPARISON OF SINGAPORE'S SKILL DEVELOPMENT FUND AND MALAYSIA'S HUMAN RESOURCE DEVELOPMENT FUND

This section compares SDF and HRDF. Nine sequential areas are examined.

Objective

In Singapore, the SDF was established in October 1979 to provide incentive grants for the development of higher skills and technology to support the economic restructuring effort. To maintain economic growth in the 1980s, the Singapore government restructured the economy by switching to higher technology and capital-intensive industries. This ensured the optimal use of manpower resources by utilising small inputs of labour in high value-added operations.

Training is considered to be an integral part of this restructuring process. While the government can educate, train and prepare fresh entrants into the labour market, the 1.1 million employed workers must be similarly prepared to take on new tasks in a restructured economy. Redundancy and retrenchment can result from structural changes in the economy but this could be pre-empted by skills development and retraining. The SDF's role, therefore, is to ensure that employers provide avenues for people already employed to acquire new or higher skills.

In Malaysia, the HRDF was established in 1 January 1993, to provide for training, retraining and skills upgrading of employees.[1] This is because the quest for the status of developed country by the year 2020 requires greater emphasis on retraining and skills upgrading of the workforce. This is necessary not only to increase the knowledge and skills intensity of the workforce but also to equip them with specialised and up-to-date skills as production techniques become increasingly more automated and complex. Retraining and skills upgrading is also of paramount importance to enhance the quality of the workforce so that it is versatile and adaptable to a changing technological and industrial environment.

---

[1] DPLT Scheme, The *Human Resources Development Act*, 1992.

Types of Skills Identified for Support

In Singapore and Malaysia, there are eight types of skills identified for priority development. These are as follows:

(i) Computer-related skills;
(ii) Craft skills;
(iii) Technical skills;
(iv) Management/supervisory skills;
(v) Professional education and specialised skills training;
(vi) R&D skills;
(vii) Company-wide productivity improvement programmes; and
(viii) Basic education for skills training.

Criteria for Support

To qualify for support in Singapore, three fundamental criteria must be met:

(i) ***Relevance to Economic Restructuring:*** This refers to Singapore's economic plan for the 1990s which focuses on higher skilled, capital-intensive operations. The emphasis is to employ labour efficiently in high value-added operations.
(ii) ***Relevance to Skills Development:*** Skills are defined as encompassing knowledge, manipulative skills and attitudes. The SDF looks for programmes which can raise the level of skills significantly. Development of simple, operative skills are excluded.
(iii) ***Relevance and Benefits to the Company:*** This means that the training must be in areas of direct benefit to their business operations.

To qualify for support in Malaysia, two fundamental criteria must be met. First, the training must be relevant to skills development. Similar to the SDF, the skills are defined as encompassing knowledge, manipulative skills and attitudes. Secondly, there must be minimum technical content in the programme. It appears that evaluation of the technical content is done on a case-by-case basis.

Level of Support

In Singapore, the amount of government subsidy towards the allowable cost ranges from 30 to 90%. The factors that determine the level of support are as follows:

(i) ***Quality of the Programme:*** Some of the factors to be considered in judging the quality and effectiveness of the training programme are:
- (a) Duration and course content in relation to the course objective;
- (b) Suitability of training approach and method of instruction;
- (c) Instructor's qualifications and experience;
- (d) Instructor/trainee ratio;
- (e) Suitability of the trainee;
- (f) Adequacy of the training facilities; and
- (g) Features that reinforce learning, like management commitment, a systematic training plan, an evaluation system and follow-up.

(ii) ***Cost Effectiveness:*** In evaluating the cost effectiveness of the programme, the following are considered:
- (a) The objective of the training and the skills developed are weighted against the investment required.
- (b) Alternative methods of developing the skills are looked at and the cost is compared. Allowance will be given for varying quality and methods.
- (c) In the case of foreign consultants, a comparison will be made with the rate charged in their home country.[2]

(iii) ***Need for Incentives:*** The SDF adopts the principle of sharing the cost of training with companies in order to ensure the companies' commitments to their training programmes. The level of support reflects the level of incentives needed for a company to make the effort to train. This is arrived at by pegging 30%, 50%, 70% or 90% support for each "allowable" cost item.[3]

In-house training programmes tailored to a company's specific needs have a greater possibility for skills application and are, therefore, more cost effective. The first-hand experience acquired through these programmes will also help build up internal training capability. Therefore, they are eligible for the highest incentive support of 90% in recognition of a company's considerable efforts and involvement.

In Malaysia, the level of support for allowable cost ranges from

---

2 DPLT Scheme, The *Human Resources Development Act*, 1992.

3 An applicant guide to the Training Grant Skill Development Fund, EDB.

30 to 90%.[4] However, there are no fundamental factors to guide the determination of the level of support. Instead, the level of financial assistance is determined by the HRD council according to Tables 9-1 and 9-2 shown below.

TABLE 9-1
Penang's Rate of Financial Assistance (above 200 employees)

Employers with 200 Employees and Above	Rates of Financial Assistance Subject to the Maximum Allowable Cost
Retraining and Skills Upgrading in Technical, Craft and Computer-Related Skills	60%
Retraining and Skills Upgrading in Quality and Productivity-Related Skills	60%
Retraining and Skills Upgrading in Supervisory Skills	60%
All Other Retraining and Skills Upgrading	40%
Overseas Training	30%

Source: DPLT Scheme, The *Human Resources Development Act,* 1992.

TABLE 9-2
Penang's Rate of Financial Assistance (below 200 employees)

Employers with 50 to 199 Employees	Rate of Financial Assistance Subject to the Maximum Allowable Costs
Retraining and Skills Upgrading in Technical, Craft and Computer-Related Skills	70%
Retraining and Skills Upgrading in Productivity-Related Skills	70%
Retraining and Skills Upgrading in Supervisory Skills	70%
All Other Retraining and Skills Upgrading	50%
Overseas Training	30%

Source: DPLT Scheme, The *Human Resources Development Act,* 1992.

Eligibility for Grants

In Singapore, to be eligible for the grants, the following two criteria must be met:

---

4 *BL Scheme Act,* 1992; The *Human Resources Development Act,* 1992.

(i) Companies have to be registered and incorporated in Singapore; and
(ii) Trainees must be employees who are either citizens or permanent residents of Singapore.

Support is not provided in the following two cases:

(i) For individuals who finance their own training programmes, partially or fully, and apply to their employers for sponsorship; and
(ii) In situations where a company bears the cost of external programmes only upon successful completion. Usually these courses are not directly related to a company's needs, and employers will provide the reimbursements under an "Education Assistance Scheme".

In Malaysia, to be eligible for the grants, the following two criteria must be met:[5]

(i) Employers must be registered and/or incorporated in Malaysia. They also must be registered with the HRD council and have contributed the HRD levy for a period of six months; and
(ii) Employees sponsored must be Malaysian citizens.

Similar to the SDF, support will not be given in the following two cases:

(i) For individuals who finance their own training programmes, whether partially or fully, and then later request their employers for sponsorship; and
(ii) Where employers will only bear the cost of training on successful completion by their employees.

Approved-in-Principle Courses

To encourage companies to have a training plan, the SDF has instituted a system of "approved-in-principle" courses. These courses are run by non-commercial organisations (e.g., NPB and SIM). In this way, employers enrolling their employees in these training courses can be assured that appropriate training grants will be given if they meet the

---

5 *SBL Scheme Act,* 1992, The *Human Resources Development Act,* 1992.

eligibility for grants.

The purpose of the approved-in-principle courses are twofold:

(i) To simplify the administration process for the courses that are frequently conducted; and
(ii) To identify courses for smaller firms to take advantage of.

For the HRDF scheme, there are also approved training programmes (ATP) similar to the approved-in-principle course in SDF. These courses under the ATP are publicly offered and need not necessarily be conducted by a government institution.

Incentive for Training

Under the SDF, there is a special incentive offered to encourage companies to develop training plans integrated with their corporate needs. This incentive takes the form of an advanced payment of the grants. Under normal conditions, grants will only be disbursed after the completion of the training programmes.

The following are three necessary conditions to qualify for advanced payment:

(i) A training plan, for at least one year, must be submitted in advance;
(ii) There must be a significant level of training activity; and
(iii) The training programme must cover at least 10% of a company's workforce.

These conditions are in addition to the normal requirement that the training programme must be relevant to economic restructuring, must be cost effective and must represent substantive skills development efforts.

Under the HRDF, there is no special advanced payment of grants incentive. Instead, there is a PLT (Pelan Latihan Tahunan) scheme where employers are encouraged to put up their annual training plans. To further assist employers, especially the smaller ones, consultants registered with the Human Resource Development Council are engaged to assist them to identify training needs, systematically formulate training programmes and prepare annual training plans.

Allowable Cost Covered

The following are the allowable costs eligible for SDF incentive grants:

(i) Course fees which are payable to the external institute or consultant;
(ii) Instructors' salary or wages of company's full-time instructors for approved in-house programmes are allowed and apportioned to the duration of training programmes. Part-time instructors, either external or staff who are paid for their instructions, will also be considered;
(iii) Absentee payroll for the wages of the trainee for the period when he is away on training. Absentee payroll is only an allowable cost item when time and productivity loss are significant;
(iv) Return airfare is allowed at economy rates only;
(v) Stipends or cost of living allowance provided by the company in addition to the trainee's salary for overseas courses. The level of support will be pegged against the company's cost or the SDF's standard rates, whichever is lower; and
(vi) Costs of new equipment to be purchased in connection with an approved training programme.

For the HRDF, the items eligible for the grants are as follows:

(i) Course fees for ATP courses or non-ATP courses by any other training providers;
(ii) Remuneration of employers' trainer(s)/instructor(s), prorated to the duration of approved in-house training programme(s): for example, four days or three and one-half days. Claims for overtime will not be allowed;
(iii) Fees paid to external trainer(s)/instructor(s) for the duration of the training programme(s);
(iv) Fees paid to foreign trainer(s)/instructor(s) for the duration of the training programme(s);
(v) Daily allowances, which include allowances for food, lodging and internal transport expenses, and which are payable to the trainee(s) for the duration of the training programme(s);
(vi) Economy rate of travelling by air; and
(vii) Consumable training materials.

Levy

For the SDF, the levy is 1% of remuneration or S$2, whichever is greater. For the HRDF, the levy is 1% of remuneration for every employee for the first and subsequent months wages commencing from the date the employer becomes liable. To demonstrate its commitment to human resources development in the country, the government will match the grant of RM$48.9 million or the amount expected to be collected in the fund's first year of operation.

CONCLUSION

From the comparison of the SDF and HRDF, it is clear that both schemes have many similarities. This is because the HRDF is modelled after the SDF. Despite the similarities, however, the HRDF is still different from the SDF in two aspects. First, the level of support for the SDF is from 30 to 90% whereas the level of support for the HRDF is from 30 to 70%. Secondly, for the SDF, the incentive scheme for a company to formulate an annual training plan is the advanced payment of grants. For the HRDF, there is a PLT scheme to assist (by means of consultancy service) a company to formulate annual training. These two differences arise because the HRDF is still developing and the fund is not large enough for a 90% level of support and advanced payment of grants. On the balance, the SDF and HRDF are effective ways in which government can intervene to correct a market failure.

OVERVIEW OF SUCCESS FACTORS

Chapter 10

Penang and Singapore: Competition or Complementarity

BY
Maria CHOW Siu Lan
HUI Choon Kit
Selene LIM Lay Hoon
SOH Leong Tat

INTRODUCTION

FROM THE REMNANTS of the Straits Settlements, via different routes, Penang and Singapore have emerged as reputable locations for certain businesses and investments. During the last few years, some businesses and manufacturing activities have been relocated from Singapore to Penang. Penang has also been sending numerous missions to Singapore for exchanges of experience.[1]

On the other hand, a number of foreign firms have chosen to invest in Penang instead of Singapore while still others have to make detailed comparative studies before deciding on their final choice of investment between the two locations.[2] Is the choice between investing in Penang versus Singapore so difficult? Before providing an answer to this question, it is necessary to consider some of the similarities and differences between Penang and Singapore.

---

1 Based on a discussion with Mr. Tan Kim Pah of the Penang Development Corporation during the MBA Business Mission.

2 Based on a conversation with Mr. Terence Chan, Managing Director, CAD-IT Consultants during the same mission.

ON STRATEGIC LOCATION

Singapore and Penang are historical and geographical trading ports along the main sea routes linking the Pacific and Indian Oceans. Both have good harbours and facilities. The support services for shipping are well-established.

By design and location, both are in the heart of one of the world's fastest growing regions. Penang enjoys direct trade with Thailand and Indonesia. As Thailand and Indonesia are fast developing, they have become big potential markets for Penang. Singapore, on the other hand, enjoys immense trade with most Asian neighbours.

ON INFRASTRUCTURE FRAMEWORK

In addition to the excellent sea transportation mentioned earlier, convenient railway links are also available to Penang and Singapore. In air transportation, Singapore has a clear advantage as it is directly linked to most of the world's big cities. Both Penang and Singapore are linked by bridges to Peninsular Malaysia. Road networks are well laid-out in both locations to facilitate the movement of goods and people.

Presently, communication facilities in Singapore are better developed than those in Penang. Singapore maintains the lead in communication as it continues to upgrade its facilities and expand its network. Penang, on the other hand, is closing up this lead at an impressive pace.

Like Singapore in the early 1970s, Penang has transformed much wasteland and poor agriculture land into industrial parks. The cost of buying or leasing land in the industrial parks in Penang is much lower than it is in Singapore.

In Penang, as in Singapore earlier, the authorities have planned and provided adequate utilities for the development of business centres and industrial parks. Investors are assured of virtually uninterrupted operations and business.

ON INCENTIVES AND GOVERNMENT POLICIES

Both the Singapore and Malaysia governments actively promote investments, especially those in the manufacturing sector. The principal tax incentives for Penang are also contained in the Malaysian *Promotion of Investment Act*, 1986, and the *Income Tax Act*, 1967. The general incentives provided by the Malaysian government to promote investments in the manufacturing sectors are the pioneer status, investment tax allowance and reinvestment allowance. In addition, special incentives are also provided by the Malaysian government to promote certain specific activities; these include export, research and development, training, storage/treatment/disposal of toxic and hazardous waste, and the establishment of operational headquarters.

The Malaysian government freely permits all payments to non-residents, including repatriation of capital and profits, subject only to the completion of a simple statistical form for remittances of more than RM10,000 each or its equivalent in foreign currency.[3] A non-resident controlled company taking up large loan amounts in Malaysia has to comply with only a few regulations.

Penang has well-located free industrial zones (FIZ) specially designed for manufacturing and assembling plants. Export oriented industries in the FIZs enjoy minimum customs control and formalities in their import of raw materials, parts, machinery and equipment, as well as in the export of their finished products.

Many of the above incentives and policies are modifications of what is available in Singapore. A manufacturing or business venture must examine its own special needs and ascertain if the existing policies in Penang or Singapore will provide an added advantage.

ON MANPOWER AND INDUSTRIAL RELATIONS

Several features characterise the workforce and labour rates in Penang. Among the more important ones are education, costs, skill levels, training and labour relations.

Educated Workforce

By Asian standards, the Singapore workforce is fairly educated. According to the Ministry of Labour's "*Report on the Labour Force Survey of Singapore 1992*", 54.4% of the 1.57 million workforce have attained a secondary or higher level of education (including post-

---

3 *Policies and Incentives*, June 1993, Penang Development Corporation.

secondary, diploma and tertiary qualifications). Another 29.9% have at least a primary or lower secondary level of education. About 8.1% of the total workforce have attained a tertiary qualification.

In 1990, 446,000 workers were employed in Penang. In a publication entitled *Statistics: Penang Malaysia* (June 1993) by the Penang Development Corporation (PDC), it is claimed that as of 1989, 60.1% of Penang's workforce had a secondary education while 31.4% had a primary level of education. Also, 4.1% of the total workforce were college/university graduates.

Both Singapore and Penang workers are proficient in the English language. Language proficiency is a competitive advantage in attracting foreign investment. In contrast, investors from the West may encounter some difficulties when communicating with the Thai or Indonesian workforce.

Labour Costs

As at 31 December 1992, out of the 146,382 persons employed in the PDC Industrial Areas, 79,455 or 54.0% (managerial, technical, supervisory and production staff included) worked in the electronics/electrical sector. Moreover, 139 factories (out of a total of 629) in the industrial areas were engaged in the manufacture of electronics/electrical products. Second in line were textiles/garment factories which employed a total of 13,940 at the end of 1992. Occupying the third position was the fabricated metal sector which employed some 10,143 workers in the same year. The rates of pay for production operators employed by major manufacturing sectors in Penang, as at 31 December 1992, are given in Table 10-1.

TABLE 10-1
Daily Wages of Skilled and Unskilled Workers in Penang

Production Operator	Electronics/ Electrical (RM)#	Fabricated Metal (RM)	Chemicals/ Fertiliser (RM)	Textiles and Garments (RM)	Plastic Products (RM)	Paper Products (RM)
Skilled	15.00*	18.50	18.00	13.50	14.00	16.00
Unskilled	12.00	12.00	12.00	10.00	10.00	10.00

\# Malaysian Ringgit
* Rate per day
Source: *Statistics: Penang Malaysia*, June 1993, PDC.

The Labour Force Survey of Singapore (1992) indicated that 433,362 workers were employed in the manufacturing sector. Out of a total of 433,362 employed (including supervisory and managerial employees), only 17,588 workers (4%) earned less than S$400 per month. Assuming 26 working days per month, the rate per day for this category of workers is S$15.40. Over 89,000 workers (approximately 21%) in this sector earned between S$600 to S$799 per month. Another 88,000 (approximately 20%) earned between S$1,000 to S$1,499 monthly. There was no indication of the skill level of workers belonging to various income brackets. Table 10-2 provides details on the breakdown of workers in the manufacturing sector by gross monthly income:

TABLE 10-2
Monthly Income of Singapore Workers

	Below S$400	**S$400 to S$599**	**S$600 to S$799**	**S$800 to S$999**	**S$1,000 to S$1,499**	**S$1,500 to S$1,999**	**S$2,000 and Above**
Gross Monthly Income	17,588	66,435	89,370	65,311	88,367	36,848	69,443
Grand Total							**433,362**

Source: Report on the Labour Force Survey of Singapore, Ministry of Labour, 1992.

One observation that can be inferred from the statistics given above is that a Singapore worker generally commands a higher wage than a Penang counterpart. The majority of Singaporeans in the manufacturing sector are earning between S$400 to $999 per month (or, S$15 to $38 per day). The highest daily wage rate a skilled worker in Penang can command is RM$18.00 (approximately S$11.00).

Skill Level

Generally speaking, about one-half of the production workers employed in Penang's major manufacturing industries including electronics, textiles and fabricated metal, are unskilled (PDC statistics). Singapore, on the other hand, has reached a stage of industrialisation where labour-intensive industries are moving out of Singapore for relocation to other neighbouring countries that have an abundant supply of cheap but unskilled labour. This relocation process is often referred to as "business migration". On its way to becoming a developed nation, Singapore has a higher proportion of skilled workers as compared to other developing countries in the region. In fact, Singapore has been providing structured technical or skill training through its polytechnics and technical institutions.

Training

One of the primary objectives of the Penang Development Corporation (PDC) is to promote the development of industry, trade and commerce. In the course of spearheading the development of industry, the PDC has been giving a lot of attention to training. With the close cooperation and understanding between the PDC and the industrialists, the Penang Skills Development Centre (PSDC) was established in 1989. The PSDC is a unique set up because it is the first human resource development training centre of its kind in the country. It is also an industry-led institution which combines the resources of its 55 members, state government and universities in designing training programmes to cater for the needs of industry.

In Singapore, similar quasi-government training or development agencies are available. The Skills Development Fund (SDF) is the classic example. The Economic Development Board (EDB) can also be considered as the counterpart of Penang's PDC. There is also the National Productivity Board (NPB) which coordinates training for the industry at a national level.

With an increasingly complex economy, Singapore has much more diversified training needs than Penang. Singapore has been, and currently is, trying to venture into carefully chosen skill-intensive or high-tech industries. The government has called on the industrialists to conduct their own in-house training. The National Wages Council (NWC) has been advising in the annual Wage Increase Guidelines that companies should allocate 4% of their payroll for training. In this sense, Singapore is moving in the direction of company-driven training.

Labour Relations

The Malaysian and Singapore labour legislations are generally similar, and in certain aspects, are almost identical. Employees' tenure is well-secured. In the case of wrongful dismissal, employees can seek redress via compensation or reinstatement. Retrenchment is legal but affected employees are given the right to negotiate for reasonable compensation.

On the other hand, management prerogatives in areas of recruitment, promotion, and transfer are also safeguarded. Both countries' labour and industrial relations legislations contribute to the "balancing" of rights and obligations between the employers and workers.

Singapore is renowned for its harmonious industrial relations and has been almost strike-free over the last two decades. The spirit of tripartite cooperation among the employers, union and government for the furtherance of national interests is deep-rooted. Since its inception in 1972, the NWC which is tripartite in composition has been playing a catalyst role in maintaining stable industrial relations.

Although strikes occur once in a while throughout the country, Penang also has harmonious industrial relations. The electronics industry, which is the largest manufacturing sector, is not unionised. Employers and human resource executives encountered during our business mission indicated that the scarcity of labour supply has enabled workers to command good wages and favourable terms of employment. Furthermore, PSDC is promoting a "caring" attitude among employers whereby companies are encouraged to commit themselves to training and human resource development.

ON POLITICAL STRUCTURE

As compared to neighbouring countries like Thailand and the Philippines, both Malaysia and Singapore enjoy relative political stability. Social unrest is virtually non-existent in Singapore and the ruling PAP has been in power since the founding of the nation. Under the able leadership of Dr. Mahathir and his associates, Malaysia is also expected to embark on a road to prosperity and stability.

A major difference in the political structure of Penang and Singapore is that the former functions within a three-tier system of local, state and federal administrations while the latter has a one-tier national government. The three-tier government structure implies that local administrators must take into consideration state as well as national priorities or interests when developing their own municipalities. The Penang Island, for example, must coordinate its development with Province Wellesley, which together, form the State of Penang.

ON COMPETITION: PENANG VERSUS SINGAPORE

Penang and Singapore share a common heritage because both were important ports of the British Malayan Straits Settlements. The similarity, however, extends beyond the good port facilities. Both locations have developed rapidly and boast of excellent infrastructure systems, well-educated and trained populations, effective legal systems adopted from the British model, and political stability. They also shared similar obstacles such as limited natural resources and land scarcity. Industrial development has generated full employment for residents of Penang and Singapore. This has led to acute labour shortages, and wages in the two locations are among the highest in ASEAN.

In response to this challenge, the Singapore government formulated the strategy of promoting only high value-added and skill-intensive industries. The labour shortage was one of the driving forces for the creation of the Singapore-Johor-Riau (Sijori) Growth Triangle. Penang has adopted a similar strategy, and is a key promoter of the much larger Indonesia-Malaysia-Thailand Growth Triangle (IMT-GT). Such a move has obviously raised some attention in Singapore.

Due to the factors mentioned earlier, Penang and Singapore have always been choice locations for foreign investors establishing operations in the Asia-Pacific region. In addition, the harmonious labour relations and attractive financial incentives offered by both locations make them even more attractive to foreign investors.

The manufacturing sector contributes substantially to Penang's GDP, and attention is presently focused on restructuring the state's manufacturing sector to make it more capital and skill-intensive. The criteria applied by the PDC in the approval of new ventures embody this principle, that is, the investments must be high value-added, capital-intensive, skill-intensive, and non-polluting industries that are able to provide forward and backward linkages. The pursuance of comparable industries by Penang and Singapore has inevitably led to some rivalry for new foreign investments.

An example of the rivalry can be inferred from the recent decision by Dornier Aerospace Company of Germany to establish an aircraft assembly and components manufacturing plant in Penang next to the Bayan Lepas International Airport. This investment was a direct result of the LIMA exhibition held on Langkawi island in December 1993. Singapore has clearly identified the aerospace industry as one of the leading sectors to be further developed. The Singapore EDB would certainly have welcomed Dornier's investment.

Based on the industries sought by Penang and Singapore as listed by the PDC and EDB, competition for investments will be keenest in the electronic, aerospace and pharmaceutical industries. Given the pro-investment climates of Penang and Singapore, foreign investors will find the evaluation to be a difficult choice. Generally, the deciding factors between the two locations are that Penang is still able to provide labour and land at much lower cost than Singapore while the latter's distinct advantages lie in a relatively better trained labour force and professional managerial expertise. Accordingly, the unit manufacturing costs in Singapore are significantly higher than in Penang for low value-added operations.

Another factor to consider is the formation of the IMT-GT which comprises the northern states of Peninsular Malaysia, south Thailand and northern Sumatra. This economic area, with its high degree of complementarity of resources, poses serious potential competition to the economy of Singapore, and which cannot be ignored. Penang has traditionally been the hub in the northern part of Peninsular Malaysia and it is the leading centre for trade, commerce, finance and education. Regional economic cooperation will definitely enhance its attractiveness to foreign investors.

ON COMPLEMENTARITY: PENANG AND SINGAPORE

Despite the competition which may arise because of similarities, there are still many areas where Singapore and Penang may complement each other due to their different stage of industrialisation. One strategy is for both locations to harness their resources in the areas in which they are strong. Singapore's strength lies in a better educated and highly skilled workforce which is trained in providing engineering based research and development services. Singapore should therefore capitalise on this comparative advantage by concentrating resources on developing higher value-added and skill-intensive activities which require personnel who are trained in research and development. Production operations which require large numbers of low skilled operators should be discouraged given the present acute labour shortage of such workers. The imposition of a high foreign worker levy by the government is meant to discourage the rampant "import" of foreign labour, and to reduce businesses reliance on foreign workers. Besides ensuring the gradual phasing out of labour-intensive industries, the government will also check prevalent social problems if the number of foreign workers is controlled.

Like Singapore, Penang is also experiencing a shortage of labour which has resulted in an escalation of labour costs. Penang tackles this problem by hiring workers from the neighbouring states and tapping into the large pool of cheap and easily available workers from countries in the IMT-GT. Given the availability of cheaper labour and land in Penang, it is cheaper for companies to set up their production plants in Penang.

A strategy which involves taking advantage of the strengths of the two locations will entail making Singapore the regional centre for research and development, and relocating production to Penang to take advantage of the cheaper land and labour. This strategy is in line with the main thrust of Singapore's and Penang's economic policies since both locations wish to be regional business and services centres.

This economic cooperation will benefit both parties in terms of higher economic growth. Besides enjoying a higher standard of living made possible by an improved economic environment, the residents of Penang will find themselves gradually trained in technical expertise, research and development skills through the transfer of technology from Singapore.

As both locations are at a different stage of development in their industrialisation programme, they are in fact not competing in many sectors of the economy. The governments of both locations are aware of their relative strengths and weaknesses, and are therefore aggressively promoting those industries which they think have a competitive advantage *vis-à-vis* other countries. For instance, Penang's manufacturing sector is the main contributor to GDP. Even though the state government is restructuring this sector to make it more capital and skill-intensive, Penang still lags behind Singapore in terms of the sophistication of technology.

With the regionalisation and globalisation of markets, economic cooperation among countries in the region to take advantage of the complementarity of resources is now the engine driving the economies of these countries. By working closely to strengthen their respective positions in the global market, instead of engaging in head-on competition, they will enlarge the "economic pie" which will result in a win-win situation for both Singapore and Penang.

CONCLUSION

As the Right Honourable Chief Minister of Penang, Dr. Koh Tsu Koon has so eloquently summarised, some competition is healthy in spurring the players to greater heights of achievement. Through working together, Penang and Singapore will be able to chart the economic growth of the Asia-Pacific and, thus, ensure that it continues to be the potential economic powerhouse of the world.

Chapter 11

Summary and Conclusion

BY
TAN Teck Meng
LOW Aik Meng
CHEW Soon Beng
John J. WILLIAMS
TAN Khee Giap

INTRODUCTION

THE DIVERSE BUSINESS interests and research studies on Penang collected from this MBA Business Mission are only to be expected since "Penang and Singapore share a common economic and historical heritage".[1] This collection is being initiated while Penang is undergoing its most exciting phase of economic transformation, especially given the current window of opportunities for greater economic cooperation amongst the sub-regions of northern Sumatra, southern Thailand and northern Malaysia. Formally known as the Indonesia-Malaysia-Thailand Growth Triangle (IMT-GT), it is a conceptual and institutional framework for the promotion of closer economic ties and linkages amongst the three sub-regions founded on the premise that "the whole is greater than the sum of its parts".[2]

Chapter 1 provided the rationale for expecting a diversity of business interests from an entrepreneurial perspective, and outlined the potential Singapore-Penang linkages. Chapter 2

[1] See speech by Dr. Cham Tao Soon, President, NTU.

[2] See speech by Dr. Ibrahim Saad, Deputy Chief Minister of Penang.

then identified characteristics of the IMT-GT which covers a physical area of 180,000 sq. km. and commands a total population of 22 million people. Although economic linkages within the IMT-GT area have existed all along with active cross-border trading, the IMT-GT was formally established only in July 1993.

Penang's economic potential, especially in terms of natural resource endowments within the IMT-GT area, relatively cheaper land for resource-based activities in both northern Sumatra and southern Thailand, and a strong across-the-board comparative advantage in labour costs from northern Sumatra, should be systematically exploited. With Penang being the most industrialised part of the growth triangle, the potential for manufacturing and industrial development must not be overlooked. The establishment of the IMT-GT, therefore, serves not only to inject a dynamic stimulus into the existing complementarity within the triangle, but it will attract further foreign investment from areas outside the triangle and most likely the ASEAN region.

Intra-regional trade could occur due to real economic complementarity, and it could also be driven by short run policy differences or distortions. Trade can take place in the form of large volume formal trade flows as well as border trade activities. Labour mobility can arise from market-driven labour flows, or flows due to general policies on foreign workers. The various crucial distinctions mentioned above, nevertheless, point to the pivotal role played by the governing authorities within the IMT-GT.

Constraints to the development of the IMT-GT can be country-specific or they can be due to general conditions prevailing within the sub-regions. The constraints can only be successfully overcome if governments within the growth triangle undertake a concerted stand on policy coordination. For instance, while relocation of labour-intensive activities to Southern Thailand and Northern Indonesia seem logical (especially for the cross-border investment in agro related industries), relocation of technological-based manufacturing activities may not be suitable at this stage given the existing level of trained workforce and infrastructure framework. On the other hand, a sub-regional centre such as Penang has great potential to evolve into the logistic and services hub of the growth triangle provided that the free flow of goods as well as the rational utilisation of infrastructure and transportation facilities are supported by the neighbouring governments. Bureaucratic national level trade policies, sub-optimal labour policies, conflicting investment policies, informal and formal barriers to foreign investment, capital funding inadequacy, and poor human resource management are just some of the prevailing hindrances or obstacles still existing in the IMT-GT which should be rationalised and rectified systematically.

Chapter 3 highlighted Penang's prospects as a regional business centre. Penang's prosperity can be attributed to the steady and robust growth of the manufacturing sector which has been, and still is, highly successful in attracting multinational corporations (MNC). In fact, this sector contributed approximately one-half of the state's gross domestic product. However, as competition for foreign investment amongst Malaysian states and within Asean countries intensifies, together with the serious threat of investment diversion looming, the strategies necessary to diversify the Penang economy become even more urgent in the 1990s.

Penang, indeed, possesses many of the basic requirements for a thriving commercial centre which include a competent workforce with high literacy, sound infrastructure, transportation facilities and dynamic growth-oriented leadership within an environment of improving political stability. To propel Penang to greater economic heights, and to greater regional economic integration, longer term investment in human resources and firm political commitment for growth are the keys to success.

Foreign direct investment serves as an important impetus to rally Penang to greater regional economic integration. Chapter 4 attempted to critically evaluate the factors and strategies that successfully have lured so many MNCs, and the ways in which Penang has benefited from their presence over the past decades. In an effort to attract foreign investors, a comprehensive range of incentives including several pioneer status, investment tax allowances, reinvestment allowances and other objectives, were carefully designed and implemented under the supervision of the Penang Development Corporation (PDC). In order to promote local enterprises, joint ventures and partnerships are being encouraged by PDC.

A significant national policy shift in terms of equity ownership between local and foreign investors, according to the export component as a proportion of total production, was introduced in the late 1980s. Such a move not only serves to promote export-oriented projects in terms of heavier investment outlay and higher value-added but it also avoids direct competition between MNCs and local enterprises.

The PDC plays an extremely important role as a one-stop investment agency for investors by providing assistance right from the initial planning stage to the final production stage. Through the PDC, potential investors to Penang benefit greatly from more transparency on incentives for investment and guidelines for the protection of foreign investment. The recent relaxation of policy on foreign and local equity ownership will also mean that market forces can now reassume their central role in the attraction of foreign direct investment.

Penang, as one of the thirteen states in Malaysia, is subject to the same tax structures, incentives and corporate reporting requirements that exist within the framework of the federal government as was documented in Chapter 5. Corporate income tax at 30% is higher in Malaysia than the 27% for Singapore which is applicable to both resident and non-resident companies. Although capital gains generally are not taxable in either Malaysia or Singapore, there is a real property gains tax ranging from 5 to 30% in the case of Malaysia, depending on the holding period of the land. It appears that on corporate tax fronts, Penang will have to do better if it is to maintain its competitiveness.

Incentives, such as capital allowances in terms of accelerated depreciation, appear to be more favourable for Singapore than Malaysia. Comparative studies also suggest that Singapore's personal income tax structure is marginally lower than that of Malaysia. As Singapore shifts its emphasis from personal income tax to a consumption tax following the introduction of the goods and services tax in April 1994, Malaysia has yet to move in this direction since the government has always encouraged thrift and saving.

Financial incentives applied to research and development (R&D) have been generous and comprehensive in Malaysia; however, progress in R&D tends to be determined by other non-financial factors such as the quality of human resources and product marketability. Incentives for export in the form of the export credit refinancing (ECR) scheme, the double deduction of export promotion expenses (EPE) and the export credit insurance premium (ECIP), are well-received in Malaysia. As Malaysia progresses steadily towards the status of a newly industrialised economy, one can expect further tax and tariff liberalisation, and an aggressive export-oriented policy drive.

Chapter 6 provided an overview of the structure of the banking system and financial markets in Penang. Banking guidelines and regulations in Penang resemble those set in the federal capital of Kuala

Lumpur where the usual capital adequacy and reserve requirements are basic requirement(s) for every licensed local financial institution.

Penang clearly has a distinct disadvantage as compared to Kuala Lumpur when it comes to rendering financial services. And, yet, Penang may be better off not to duplicate Kuala Lumpur as a financial centre. Instead, Penang should concentrate on specialised funding requirements and speedy facilities for trade and investment purposes. In other words, Penang may be more suited to a regional commercial hub rather than a regional financial centre.

Penang started the industrialisation drive much earlier than did the rest of Malaysia with particular emphasis given to the manufacturing sector. With an estimated population of about 1.1 million, labour force participation and industrial employment turnover are intimately linked as was discussed in Chapter 7.

The labour participation rate was estimated at 63.4% in 1990 with the male and female populations constituting 86% and 44.5%, respectively. Over 95% of the labour force is employed in various industries, and almost one-half of those are working in the manufacturing sector. Employment is projected to grow from the rate of 5.1% in 1993–94 to 8.5% in 1994–95. It is hardly surprising that an overall labour turnover rate of 48.2% was recorded for the year 1992–93 with some industrial sectors reporting a 60% turnover rate. Clearly such trends point towards the inevitable situation of a tightening labour supply caused by a strong demand for unskilled workers in particular.

The supply side constraint of the labour market, in turn, slows down the manufacturing sector's activities thus forcing businesses to turn to cheaper and more abundant sources of labour. The alternative, of course, is to move up the technological ladder by investing in labour saving automated machinery and equipment which could be a costly adjustment process even for successful enterprises. Although the influx of labour from other states of northern Malaysia helps to alleviate the tight labour market situation somewhat, workers are attracted by intense competition from neighbouring industrialising states such as central and southern Malaysia which offer higher wages.

Remedies to reduce labour turnover, given the labour force participation rate in Penang, called for a market-oriented approach of paying better for skilled labour and relocating labour intensive industries to other sub-regions of the growth triangle. A longer term approach would include having the private sector involved in setting up the Human

Resource Development Fund (HRDF), and also drawing out a comprehensive Skill Development Programme (SDP) where workers can acquire new skills, and can be retrained through various incentive programmes.

The resiliency of the industrialisation drive of Penang depends largely on the ability to keep wage costs down and, in particular, wage costs of the manufacturing sector since it contributes about 46% of the state's GDP, and 46% of the employment created in the 1990s. It appears that despite the tight labour market condition, comparative studies of the average wage costs between Penang and Singapore revealed that average salaries for engineers, technicians and skilled production workers of the former still range just one-third to one-quarter of those being paid in Singapore. However, such observed divergences in the levels of salaries may be misleading if labour legislation, trade unions and the wage determination process in Penang are not considered.

Chapter 8, therefore, examined the statutory provisions and collective agreements in Penang. It also reviewed the industrial relations system and the collective wage bargaining process. Malaysian workers are not highly unionised since they consist of about 10% of those eligible to be union members. Such a trend may be the result of deliberate attempts by companies to discourage workers from joining unions by offering, instead, positive long term incentives and welfare. However, with the high employment turnover in the industrial sector, such proactive attempts by companies can hardly be regarded as very successful.

In any case, Malaysian industrial relations operate on a tripartite system which includes the employer, the employees and the government, and they go through essentially the same collective bargaining process as that of Singapore. Looking at the statutory benefits/provisions being included in the collective agreements, it seems that Malaysians have more specific provisions and more thorough coverage than Singaporeans although such advantages may not necessarily translate into better or more favourable conditions for employees. However, given the current state of near full employment in Penang, employers see the need to collaborate with employees for mutual benefits. Industrial relations are harmonious in Penang and the old confrontation tactics seem out of date.

In view of the rapid industrialisation over the past two decades, manpower shortages and mismatches between job requirements and labour skills are some of the serious problems to be solved. The Penang government has since adopted several highly successful skills development strategies some of which were discussed in Chapter 9. Manpower training and development was first initiated and provided for by the Penang Skill Development Centre (PSDC). Incentives to employers for supporting the upgrading of skills and productivity improvement of the workforce came in the form of double deduction for expenditures on training, Human Resources Development Fund (HRDF) assistance and Industrial Building Allowance (IBA). PSDC adopts a four-prong approach in skill development strategies by developing technical skills, fostering industry cooperation in training, coordinating formal and informal training arrangements with federal ministries, and re-establishing Penang as a regional centre for manpower training and development.

Malaysia's HRDF basically plays a similar role to that of the Skills Development Fund (SDF) of Singapore in terms of objectives, types of skills supplied, level and criteria for cost support, since the former is modelled after the latter. On the whole, SDF and HRDF are effective ways by which government can assume a proactive role to correct for market failures.

Having studied the industrial development process, understood the various detailed aspects of the economy, identified the critical success factors and future potential of Penang as a regional commercial hub, one frequent circumspection that tends to be raised is whether Penang's robust pace of growth poses direct competition for Singapore in the near future?

Chapter 10 examined Singapore and Penang from a broad macro political-economic perspective since the two island economies do possess similarities and a common ground in terms of physical size, strategic location, historical heritage, infrastructure framework, human resources management, industrial relations and development objectives. It is acknowledged that Singapore is far ahead of Penang, and the latter looks upon the former as a "benchmark" for development but with slight variations in approach.[3]

In order not to be engaged in a defensive mood of maintaining competitiveness by conceding more concessions and offering more incentives, both Penang and Singapore can look beyond their existing

---

[3] See speech by Dr. Koh Tsu Koon, Chief Minister of Penang.

boundaries and project themselves into new emerging markets in the neighbouring regions. Such visions would call for a joint effort to synergise resources and to spot market niches based on each one's respective strengths and aspirations.[4]

Finally, the perceived areas of competition and the areas of complementarity between Penang and Singapore were outlined. In conclusion, a win-win situation appears eminent whereby Penang and Singapore work closely to strengthen their respective positions in emerging markets. Of course, to enlarge their economic pies, some competition is deemed healthy in spurring the two players to greater heights of achievement which would be optimal for everyone.

---

4 See speech by Dr. Koh Tsu Koon, Chief Minister of Penang.

SEMINAR ON "INVESTMENT OPPORTUNITIES IN PENANG"

KEYNOTE ADDRESS BY THE RIGHT HONOURABLE DR. KOH TSU KOON, CHIEF MINISTER OF PENANG 20 JULY 1993

I am very pleased to be given this opportunity to deliver the Keynote Address for the Seminar on "**Investment Opportunities in Penang**". I must thank our good friends in the Singapore Manufacturers Association, particularly your President, Mr. Robert Chua, MIDA Singapore, and Singapore Trade Development Board for their assistance in staging this Seminar with the Penang Development Corporation.

Let me take this opportunity to welcome each and everyone of you who have taken valuable time off your business schedules to be present here this morning. I am sure that the presentations by the PDC and MIDA will give you a better insight into the opportunities that await you in Penang.

In this Age of "Global Village", where communication has brought the world that much closer in terms of travel time and the ease of communication by the various media, the need for strategic alliances will grow even more. In the case of Penang and Singapore, our cultural and historical ties can be further cemented through economic cooperation. We are confident of forging a win-win relationship where there are no losers but only winners.

Our seminar today is aimed at forging closer links with Singapore — beyond the goodwill and friendship visits between our leaders. Our focus is on economic development and on industrialisation and I believe that there is a lot which can be achieved if we work together. We are looking at complementing the advantages of both locations so that the benefits will accrue to both parties. Joint ventures with Singapore manufacturers in supportive and ancillary industries, parallel and supplementary manufacturing activities for MNCs, service industries, business consultancy, and trading activities are some of the many opportunities that Penang can offer. We are confident that the Penang-Singapore relationship can be carried to the next plane of economic cooperation.

In an economic environment that changes rapidly, there is always a tendency first to hinge on the familiar, to expand and then to move on to take on new frontiers. In this context, we look at Singapore as familiar old friends. We have a somewhat similar historical background including the Straits Settlements and British rule, almost similar administrative and legislative set-ups and, I believe, even similar development objectives. I must admit, however, that you are far ahead of us and we look upon you as a "benchmark" for development but with slight variations so that our approach is more Malaysian.

Indeed, there is a need for us to look beyond the scope of our own boundaries and, yet, not to be too overawed by new emerging boundaries. New frontiers need to be found and new markets need to be created to support our ever expanding manufacturing base. AFTA or the Asean Free Trade Area, is borned out of the realisation that the South-east Asian region is the fastest growing in the world and that our destiny lies in our own hands.

We are looking at a population of 475 million people in the South-east Asian region, a young, energetic, increasingly affluent and middle class population who demand a quality of life comparable, if not better, than that of the developed nations. This discerning group of people form the bulk of our consumer population and they will demand goods and services which are cost competitive, environmentally friendly and give value for money. Meeting their needs represents a challenge to the manufacturing and trading communities in this region.

We are not talking of an inwardly looking economy, with emphasis on expanding the "local" market where local means ASEAN. We need to eventually look at the world market where standards are set and technology is current. We need to have a better grasp of changing consumer tastes. It puts a new meaning to the term "think global, act local".

Penang which started by attracting MNCs to establish manufacturing facilities, will now be more selective, more discerning and more focused in its next stage of industrialisation. After 20 years, we have built a good foundation upon which to springboard to meet our national aspirations of an industrialised country by the year 2020. We now give emphasis to promoting high value-added activities which will require higher capital, technological and skill content. We encourage ancillary and support industries as well as activities that will help to develop better linkages with other sectors and between our local entrepreneurs and the MNCs.

Our market niches in the area of manufacturing are the MNCs and the supportive and ancillary industries which are growing together from strength to strength. We are targeting MNCs which are looking at good supportive and ancillary industry back up, are generally less labour-intensive, need good infrastructure and would like to take advantage of access to an increasingly large and sophisticated market. Our 20 years of experience in international manufacturing has resulted in a workforce which is high on skills and has the ability to learn and adapt quickly.

Penang will be viewed favourably by companies involved in electronics, precision machining, computer peripherals, related upstream and downstream activities, R&D activities and generally companies that see ASEAN, and subsequently the Asian region, as their expanding market. Similarly, companies that carry out high value-added activities and which utilise local primary resources will want to take advantage of our skilled worker base and the availability of incentives for such industries.

We realise that to achieve our goals for the next stage of industrialisation that I have just outlined, we need to inform new investors of our plus factors and attract industrial, commercial and service-oriented operations that we have targeted.

The strategic geographical position of Penang; a stable government; excellent, well-developed and modern infrastructural facilities; a quality of life that is comparable with the developed nations; an intelligent, disciplined, hardworking and dedicated labour force; and favourable incentives for the investors are all key factors that explain how Penang has long been, and will continue to be, a major attraction for investors.

The overall economic stability and growth, together with a capable administrative and political leadership, will certainly provide a conducive climate for investment. We also have an active private sector to complement the investment opportunities for a thriving manufacturing sector.

We have amidst our delegation from Penang members from the private sector, particularly those in the ancillary and support industries, who are capable of meeting the needs of MNCs. We hope that you will make use of their presence to exchange notes and views which will give you added insights into the data and information that will be discussed by the PDC and MIDA officials. While such data are important, I am sure that you will also want to hear the views of your counterparts and learn first hand from them how business is being done and what governmental support has been given for example.

Over the next decade, Penang will surge forward to foster an increasingly dynamic, progressive and resilient economy. We will adopt strategies to broaden and deepen the economic base through the promotion and development of the other sectors. Within the manufacturing sector, we will promote an R&D culture and the establishment of a high-tech environment. We will continuously upgrade the State's technological capabilities to establish Penang as the regional centre for technology in northern Peninsular Malaysia and the Indonesia-Malaysia-Thailand Growth Triangle (IMT-GT). To achieve this objective, we will encourage international companies to set up their regional engineering and technical centres in Penang. In light of the present economic development of the Asia Pacific Rim, Penang is well-positioned to play a significant role as a centre of excellence within the context of a regional industrial and technology centre.

We realise that as Penang moves into an era of high-technology manufacturing and support services, the development of skilled human resources becomes a key issue. By recognising the importance of training, the State Government has taken steps to initiate educational and training programmes compatible with the requirements of the industries. Penang is the first state to set up a Human Resource Development Council (HRDC) which pools the contributions and resources of the private sector and the public sector to map out and plan for greater human resource development programmes.

We believe in working together with the private sector to plan for, and implement, programmes that will bring greater benefits to our parties. Training organisations such as the Penang Skills Development Centre (PSDC), the Plastic Technology Training Centre and the proposed Penang Timber-based Furniture Training and Design Centre are some of the combined initiatives of the public and private sectors aimed at upgrading the skill levels of our people.

These initiatives are augmented by the formal education programmes provided by private sector groups such as the Kolej Damansara Utama (KDU), Disted College, Cyma College and the new PIETC (Penang International Education and Technology Centre) which will offer post graduate and graduate studies in business management and information technology. We see Penang re-emerging as an important education centre to serve the needs of the four northern States of Peninsular Malaysia and the IMT-GT.

Education and training are essential to prepare our people to work in a modern and high-technology manufacturing environment. It is only through training and re-training that we can achieve high productivity and zero defects performance.

What I have just outlined are some of the very key areas that the government has identified and to achieve our objectives it has worked out action plans to prepare Penang to play host to even more technology, skill, and knowledge intensive industries.

There is constantly talk of competition amongst investment centres with each one trying to outbeat the others by offering greater concessions and better incentives. I feel that we need to consolidate our efforts jointly so as to ensure synergy. We need to identify market niches based on our respective strengths and the aspirations of our people. We can then play complementary and supplementary roles and ensure that we derive the maximum benefits from our industrial promotion efforts.

This calls for belief and commitment in the greater and bigger objectives of regional growth and efficiency in the utilisation of resources. We feel that this is the way to go and to allow the free flow of resources between growth centres is a start towards achieving this natural balance in development.

In this context, we encourage joint ventures which will synergise our resources. Joint ventures are especially effective when there is a marriage of good ideas, technological back-up, understanding of local conditions and market niches. The availability of any one of these four factors can make a good joint venture partner. Looking at the increasing opportunities for supporting and ancillary services, the need to provide just-in-time services, and the ever changing local manufacturing scenario, it makes a lot of sense for Singapore companies to interface with their Penang counterparts and forge these important joint ventures.

I would, therefore, like to invite you to grow with us in unison by setting up manufacturing facilities and business ventures in Penang. After all, Singapore and Penang are only an hour's flight time apart. If we combine our strengths, then we certainly have a bright future ahead. We should view ourselves as partners in progress. There is much to be gained and I am sure that you will not regret your decision and wisdom to site your operation in Penang.

Thank you, and have a fruitful discussion with the State officials and private sector members. Let this seminar be the prologue for better things to come for us all.

CLOSING DINNER OF ENDEC WORLD CONFERENCE ON ENTREPRENEURSHIP

SPEECH BY THE RIGHT HONOURABLE DATUK DR. IBRAHIM SAAD, DEPUTY CHIEF MINISTER OF PENANG

AT MARINA MANDARIN SINGAPORE ON 8 JULY 1994, 7.30 PM

"INDONESIA-MALAYSIA-THAILAND GROWTH TRIANGLE(IMT-GT): OPPORTUNITIES AND PROSPECTS"

I am indeed honoured to have been given this privilege to speak to such a distinguished audience on a subject that has evoked a lot of interest recently, not only amongst politicians and bureaucrats but, also, amongst academicians and entrepreneurs.

In this respect, I would like to thank the Entrepreneurship Development Centre, or ENDEC, of Nanyang Technological University which is the organiser of this Conference for giving me this opportunity to address all of you on the subject of the Indonesia-Malaysia-Thailand Growth Triangle, or IMT-GT for short.

The IMT-GT attempts to provide both the conceptual and institutional framework for the promotion of closer economic ties and linkages amongst the sub-regions of northern Sumatra, northern Peninsular Malaysia and southern Thailand. Conceptually, it is not any different from other forms of regional economic cooperation in that it is founded on the premise that "the whole is greater than the sum of its parts".

Geographically, the IMT-GT encompasses the provinces of northern Sumatra and Acheh in Indonesia, the northern Peninsular Malaysian States of Kedah, Penang, Perak and Perlis as well as the five provinces of Narathiwat, Satun, Songkhla, Pattani and Yala in southern Thailand.

Collectively, the IMT-GT region has a geographical area of 180,137 square kilometres and a combined population of 21 million. It is significant that the population profile of the three countries is relatively young as compared to the industrialised nations of the West. It is even more significant that while some of the Western industrialised nations are suffering from low rates of economic expansion, it is generally acknowledged that the Asia-Pacific region will be the focus of economic activity in the 21st century.

Within the Asia-Pacific region, it cannot be denied that one of the most promising regions is ASEAN. All the ASEAN countries, including the member countries of the IMT-GT, have recorded very robust rates of growth for most of the last decade with some in the double-digit range. The increasing prosperity of ASEAN, particularly the IMT-GT members, and the accompanying increase in the standard of living of our people means that there is likely to be a steady increase in the demand for goods and service within the region itself.

However, I would like to suggest that it would be myopic for anyone to look at the prospects of the IMT-GT in isolation. I strongly believe that the IMT-GT should be viewed in the larger context of the global trend towards liberalisation of trade and investment as symbolised by the recent international accord under the auspices of the General Agreement on Tariffs and Trade (GATT). At the regional level, the implementation of the Asean Free Trade Area (AFTA) accord, reached in January 1992, will also enhance trade and investment flows amongst ASEAN countries through the progressive reduction of tariff barriers over a 15-year time frame.

Conceptually, then, one can describe this scenario as being symbolised by three concentric circles: the innermost circle representing the IMT-GT; the next circle representing AFTA; and the outermost circle representing GATT. Seen within this context, the IMT-GT represents a very fundamental and significant attempt at promoting intra-regional and inter-regional flows of trade and investment so that all of us in the developing countries may be able to promote economic growth endogenously, thereby reducing our economic dependence on the Western industrialised nations.

However, one should not misconstrue this statement as implying that the members of the IMT-GT should be inward-looking. On the contrary, the IMT-GT countries should be outward-looking and export-oriented so that they may be able to accelerate their rate of economic growth by satisfying the needs of global markets. It should be emphasised that this outward-looking export orientation ought to be accompanied by the harmonisation of domestic policies and procedures of IMT-

GT member countries. This will enable them to use their resources collectively to the best advantage by bringing together their complementarities and thereby promoting synergistic growth of the region as whole.

Having outlined the conceptual framework and the *raison d'etre* for the IMT-GT my optimism is not only derived from the complementarities that exist amongst the IMT-GT countries but, more importantly, it is also derived from the political commitment of the three national governments towards this concept. The IMT-GT concept was formalised at a ministerial meeting of the three governments at Langkawi on 20 July 1993. Although less than a year has passed since the formal adoption of the IMT-GT concept and, thus, it could be described as being in its infancy, there is not an *iota* of doubt that there is political commitment at the highest level in each of the three countries. This is demonstrated by the fact that although the Asian Development Bank had been appointed by the three governments to undertake a study with a view to identifying suitable areas for trilateral and bilateral cooperation, the governments have seen fit to adopt certain decisions and implement programmes of action immediately while awaiting the completion of the Asian Development Bank study.

Even at the inaugural meeting of the IMT-GT in July 1993, the three governments had agreed that they would like to foster and promote co-operation in certain areas. These included the joint promotion of tourism, agro-processing and fruit cultivation, the relocation of labour-intensive aspects of the electronics industries in Penang to southern Thailand and northern Sumatra, the establishment of rubber-wood processing mills in southern Thailand and the export of expertise by Malaysian Industrial Estates Ltd through the development of industrial estates in northern Sumatra and southern Thailand.

Although there is political commitment at the highest level and the three governments are prepared to review domestic policies and procedures, both in the interest of uniformity and trade liberalisation, they have nevertheless recognised that the initiative for business undertakings rests squarely with private enterprise. While the governments can formulate enabling policies and procedures, and can even assist in identifying suitable areas for co-operation through the Asian Development Bank study, it is incumbent upon the private sector to identify specific business opportunities and work together with their counterparts in the other two countries so as to realise the full potential of the IMT-GT for the mutual benefit of everyone.

In this respect, it is important that there be a continuing dialogue not only amongst the three governments at both the national and provincial levels but, more importantly, amongst the members of the business community. Thus, the three governments also have agreed that a joint business council be established to promote greater rapport and interaction amongst the business leaders of the three participating countries.

Within Malaysia, the four northern states of Kedah, Penang, Perak and Perlis have established an IMT-GT liaison office in Alor Star, Kedah. Although initially it was envisaged that this liaison office would coordinate the responses of the four northern states within the IMT-GT framework, it has recently been proposed that this liaison office be upgraded to an information and promotion centre for the whole IMT-GT region. If this proposal is realised, then this liaison office will maintain a database on economic activities in each of the participating countries as well as the investment incentives and other information of interest to any potential investor. Where it is possible, the office also will promote the IMT-GT region as a whole.

I realise that as Singaporeans, you are interested to know the opportunities that are available to you within the IMT-GT framework. As I have stated earlier, the IMT-GT is still in its infancy and even the Asian Development Bank study on prospective areas of co-operation has not been completed yet. Notwithstanding that, I would like to emphasise that we are very open-minded and we are prepared to consider any proposal or suggestion that may emanate from you. I also would like to highlight that the three governments have agreed that a project need not involve all the countries in order to come within the ambit of the IMT-GT. It can be considered an IMT-GT project even if it involves only two of the participating countries.

Finally, I would like to say that the long term prospect for the IMT-GT is indeed very bright given the rapid expansion of the economies of the whole region, the political commitment of the participating governments, and the increasing trend towards liberalisation of trade and investment. However, the only caveat to this optimism is that all of us must be able to rise above narrow nationalistic perceptions and work towards win-win situations for the benefit of all concerned.

After all, the IMT-GT is only building upon trade that has historically existed amongst the participating countries. Penang was the entrepot centre for much of the produce of southern Thailand and parts of Indonesia. However, the IMT-GT focuses our attention on the tremendous potential benefits that all of us can derive if only we adopt a regional approach to development, thus transcending national boundaries.

I hope that I have at least been successful in evoking some interest in the IMT-GT for the participants here. In the event that any of you would like to pursue any proposals, you are most welcome to contact us in Penang.

Thank you.

MBA BUSINESS MISSION TO PENANG, MALAYSIA
23 – 27 FEBRUARY 1994

CLOSING BANQUET SPEECH
DR. CHAM TAO SOON,
PRESIDENT, NANYANG TECHNOLOGICAL UNIVERSITY
25 FEBRUARY 1994

Dr. Koh Tsu Koon, Chief Minister of Penang, Dr. Ibrahim Saad, Deputy Chief Minister of Penang, distinguished guests, ladies and gentlemen.

Penang and Singapore share a common economic and historical heritage. Our strategic geographical locations have placed us at the cross-roads for trade between East and West as early as the 1800s. In 1826, the British declared the existing colonies of Penang, Malacca and Singapore as the Straits Settlements to protect the commercial and political interests of the British in the East.

Since then, the relations between Penang and Singapore have been good. Singapore ranks sixth in terms of foreign investment in Penang. In July 1993, an investment seminar promoting Penang was organised in Singapore. The high-powered Penang delegation led by Chief Minister Koh was well-received by Singapore businessmen. On 21 January 1994, the Deputy Minister of Penang, Dr. Ibrahim Saad, visited the Nanyang Technological University under the Lee Kuan Yew Exchange Fellows Programme. We were impressed by the measures taken by you to promote Penang as an ideal investment location, and by your rapid economic growth, and decided that Penang should be the venue for our sixth MBA Business Mission.

Our previous business missions had taken us to Jakarta, Bangkok, Malacca, Xiamen in China and Ho Chi Minh City in Vietnam. Those business missions have resulted in some business deals. For instance, one of our MBA participants has set up a boutique hotel in Malacca. Another MBA participant secured an important business project in Xiamen after participating in the MBA business mission to Xiamen. This project is now so big that he has to take leave of absence from the MBA programme. On the first day of our business mission here in

Penang, we were privileged to be invited to the Official Opening of CAD-IT Consultants (M) Sdn Bhd. This company was started by Mr. Terence Chan who is a graduate from our pioneer batch of MBA participants.

The MBA Business Mission to Penang symbolises the importance that NTU places on the efforts of your government in promoting regional bilateral trade and investment between Penang and Singapore. I am very confident that our MBA participants, some of whom are senior managers in both the private and the public sectors and some of whom are entrepreneurs, will find this business mission to Penang very useful in establishing friendship and networking that will be invaluable to their future business dealings in Penang.

On behalf of NTU, I would like to express my appreciation to the Chief Minister of Penang, the Deputy Chief Minister of Penang and the Penang Development Corporation for their hospitality and generosity, and for making this business mission to Penang a memorable and educational experience for our participants.

Thank you.

FEEDBACK FORM

Thank you for purchasing the Nanyang Business Report series. In order to aid us with the development of other similar books in the future, please give us your opinion in this form and fax or mail it to us at the address given on the back. We would also like to include your name in our mailing list to keep you informed of book promotions which we may have in the future.

Name: ____________________ Occupation: ____________________

Company: ____________________ Type of business: ____________________

Address: ____________________

____

Do you normally purchase this kind of book? ❑ Yes ❑ No

Which title did you buy? ____________________

Why? ____________________

How did you learn about this book? ❑ courses/seminars ❑ recommended text

❑ bookshop ❑ advertisements ❑ Others(please specify) ____________________

What business magazines are you subscribing to? ____________________

____

What seminars do you normally attend? ____________________

What suggestions for improvement would you recommend to the book you bought?

____

____

What kind of areas do you think we should focus on in business publishing?

____

Why? ____________________

____

Would you like to be part of our direct mail/mailing list? ❑ Yes ❑ No

Please list out subject areas ____________________

Would you like to aid us in our publishing decision by being a reviewer of unpublished works? ❑ Yes ❑ No

Please list out subject areas if different from above ____________________

____

Please fax to:

The Managing Editor, Simon & Schuster (Asia) Pte Ltd, fax: 3780 371 or email your response to prenhall@singnet.com.sg

FOLD HERE

FOLD HERE

AFFIX STAMP

The Managing Editor
Simon & Schuster (Asia) Pte Ltd
317 Alexandra Road
#04-01 IKEA Building
Singapore 159965